To Caithm
Enjoy!
Best wishes
Tom Harris 29.9.11

Why I'm right ...
and everyone else is wrong

The best of the blog

Tom Harris

Biteback Publishing

First published in Great Britain in 2011 by
Biteback Publishing Ltd
Westminster Tower
3 Albert Embankment
London
SE1 7SP

ISBN 978-1-84954-105-3

10 9 8 7 6 5 4 3 2 1

A CIP catalogue record for this book is available from the British Library.

Set in Adobe Caslon Pro by Soapbox

Printed and bound in Great Britain by
CPI Group (UK) Ltd, Croydon, CR0 4YY

Contents

Introduction

It was exactly ten o'clock at night and the division bell was signalling a vote in the Commons. Dutifully I headed towards the 'aye' lobby. There are two ways to get into the 'aye' lobby if you're walking from the direction of the Members' Lobby: you can either queue up the stairs on the left hand side of the chamber or you can walk the length of the chamber, past the government despatch box and the Treasury bench, and enter through the main lobby doors behind the Speaker's chair.

I don't queue.

And as I headed leisurely towards the table on which the royal mace sat, I came face to face with the Chancellor of the Exchequer, Gordon Brown.

At this point I had known Gordon for about sixteen years. He was the shadow Trade and Industry Secretary when I was appointed the Scottish Labour Party's first ever full-time press officer. And, like him, I was a member of the Scottish group of Labour MPs, though admittedly my membership was only five years old.

So I think I had every right to expect him to know my name, right?

He paused as he was about to walk past me. He glowered (I'm taller than him, so why did I always get the feeling he was glowering *down* at me?) and I could see that two things were occurring: first, he regretted pausing and thereby committing himself to a conversation that he didn't really want to have and, secondly, he knew he ought to recognise me but was clearly having a hard time placing me.

Suddenly his mouth quivered in triumph (relief?) as the pieces fell into place and a light went on somewhere inside his brain.

'I saw the questions you put down on Crossrail. Douglas and I are going to give you a good answer.'

Oh, where to start, where to start…?

First of all, 'Douglas' was Douglas Alexander, the transport secretary. Fair enough. The slight problem was that I was in no position to table questions on Crossrail – the proposed new commuter railway line running across central London – since I was, at the time, the minister responsible for… oh, what was it again…? Ah, yes, Crossrail!

Not only was I responsible for the scheme in my capacity as the Parliamentary Under-Secretary of State at the Department for Transport, I had, just a few months earlier, had a telephone conversation with Gordon during which he brought up the subject of funding for the scheme.

And here we were, a short time later, with only a few weeks left of Tony Blair's premiership, with Gordon reportedly nervous about the possible emergence of a challenge to his 'right' to take over from Tony … this was his way of courting the Parliamentary Labour Party.

And he couldn't even remember who the hell I was.

Now, there were three ways I could have responded to this uninvited and useless piece of information proffered by the Chancellor:

a. *Thanks, Gordon.*
b. *Thanks, Gordon, but I'm actually the minister responsible for Crossrail, so I'm the one who'll be issuing the answer to any questions tabled by back benchers, thank you very much.*
c. *Thanks, David.*

Being a coward, I chose option (a). Option (b) would have embarrassed both of us and it's said GB bears grudges, so it was probably sensible to reject that one. Option (c), in hindsight, would have been the most amusing, probably worth curtailing my ministerial career for.

I mention this little anecdote at the start of this book mainly because it's this kind of thing that made my blog, *And Another Thing…*, so successful during the two and half years in which I published it (though this is the first time I've retold the tale publicly).

But the other reason I retell it now is because Gordon Brown became the pivotal political figure in the period of my life when the blog was on the go. He was always there, somewhere, often in the background, often not, defining the political events of that period. When he sacked me in October 2008 he had quite a significant role in shaping my personal life, one way or the other.

The three years of his premiership were, on the whole, not a happy time for me, for my party or for my country. Nor, I suppose, for Gordon, much of the time. History, I regret to say, will judge him harshly, though not as harshly as those of us in the Parliamentary Labour Party who came bitterly to regret his machinations and systematic undermining of Tony Blair.

And for what? A good friend and colleague who supported Gordon's coup against Tony in September 2006 told me recently of his disappointment with our former leader: 'He tried so hard to get to the top and when he got there, there was nothing there, he had nothing to offer.'

As for me, I am proud of my political epitaph: 'Appointed by Tony Blair, sacked by Gordon Brown.'

But this is not an insider's account of Labour's path to self-destruction at the 2010 general election. Indeed, in the blog I only gave occasional glimpses of my unhappiness with Gordon's leadership. And quite right too – I was not going to allow myself to be blamed for the looming and inevitable electoral catastrophe by being blatantly disloyal online.

So, instead, the blog became an exercise in self-restraint and discipline in how to write in an interesting and even loyal way about politics during the most difficult period of Labour's thirteen years in government.

You don't want more opinions about why political blogging is important, about why I started blogging, about the impact of blogging on the world of politics or any of that nonsense, do you? You already have your own opinions about all that stuff, so why bother?

No, what you want is gossip. The reason *And Another Thing...* was relatively successful is because it gave readers an insight into the life – political and personal – of an MP. That in itself was a unique selling point: who knew that MPs had family lives, favourite TV programmes and bands, even a sense of humour?

In this book I've collected together the posts of which I'm most proud, as well as those which, for one reason or another, gained a certain degree of national notoriety. Rather than list them chronologically, I've chosen to do it by category, so that those readers who, for whatever inexplicable reason, are not fans of, say, *Doctor Who*, can skip past those bits and head straight for the politics.

I wrote *And Another Thing...* for two and a half years, from March 2008 until November 2010, usually updating two, sometimes three or four, times every day. That's a lot of blogging. I was frequently challenged about the wisdom of devoting so much of my time as an MP to the task. With hindsight, I would say it was time well spent if it meant engaging with the public, and promoting ideas and values which I thought – which I still think – are important.

The danger with being so upfront about my views – about being unapologetically New Labour and a devotee of Tony Blair's – is that one quickly understands just how popular such positions are within the post-2010 Labour Party. Which is to say, not very.

And when you've lost the argument, and when no one in your own party is supporting you, except by whispering 'Well done' in the voting lobby when the whips aren't watching, you have to conclude that there might be better ways of spending your time.

Parliament

Those who can't, write
Published: June 26, 2008

Fraser Nelson was predictably cruel in his comments about Khalid Mahmood's question yesterday at Prime Minister's Questions: 'He stuttered, gasped, looked at his papers. How difficult can it be to ask one question?' Well, you'll never know the answer to that, Fraser, but believe me, it's a lot harder than it looks, and certainly a lot harder than sitting in your office criticising the efforts of others.

Asking a question – any question – at PMQs is surely the most daunting of experiences. For a start, there are nearly three hundred people opposite who are positively willing you to fail. And that's before you even consider that you're being watched on live TV throughout the land. You're also aware that there are reporters in the gallery ready to snipe and sneer at the first sign of a stumble. And on top of that, there's a huge amount of pressure from your own supporters who desperately want you to succeed. Writing a blog or a column is a cake walk next to that.

As a back bencher I asked the (previous) PM a number of questions on a range of subjects, from child benefit and apprenticeships to drugs and knife crime, although the only one people remember was on light pollution, in 2003. Having instigated the Science and Technology Select Committee inquiry into the effects of light pollution on astronomy, I stood up to ask 'When was the last time the Prime Minister had a clear view of the Milky Way galaxy?'

All. Hell. Broke. Loose.

The opposition started bawling and shouting, our side started cheering; an awful din. The only thing to do was plough on (no pun intended). I got to the end of the question without stumbling or forgetting my line and – crucially – without being called out of order by the Speaker for taking too long. I had been well and truly bloodied. I felt exhilarated. But it could so easily have gone wrong. It often does and, frankly, no journalist who has not experienced it himself, and who therefore has no grasp of the pressures individuals

Nothing whatever to do with All-Bran

Published: February 12, 2009

I tabled an Early Day Motion (EDM) the day before yesterday, the first time I've done so for a long time.

They're interesting things, EDMs. Most, if not all, MPs receive countless requests from constituents every week requesting that they sign this or that EDM. Only backbench MPs can sign. This is more than a convention; if you're a whip or a minister you're actually prevented from having your name against a motion. When I was appointed as a minister in September 2006, I received a letter from the Table Office in the House of Commons informing me that my name had consequently been removed from every EDM I had previously been supporting.

Many backbenchers, however, refuse to sign EDMs at all. Depending on your perspective, this allows them to have an 'equal opportunities' policy towards all their constituents; alternatively it could be seen as a policy that disappoints every constituent who wants to see his or her MP support a particular cause. Parliamentary Private Secretaries (PPSs), although technically (unpaid) members of the government, sometimes sign EDMs, though can't sign those that criticise the government or that call for a change in policy.

But what do they actually achieve? Very little, if you want to take the cynical approach. They're almost never debated (not while I've been an MP, anyway). However, they can serve as a useful temperature gauge of MPs' views in certain policy areas; ministers sit up and take note when any motion starts to gain the support of more than 100 or so MPs.

And they're one of the few mechanisms that the public have for having a say, albeit indirectly. There are certainly more than a few EDMs which I probably wouldn't have signed had constituents not drawn them to my attention.

But their importance shouldn't be overstated, and constituents shouldn't be too disappointed if their MP informs them he or she can't support a particular EDM.

In the run-up to war in Iraq, the comedian Mark Steel tried to suggest that Tony Blair had, in the 1980s, ignored the plight of the Iraqi Kurds who were massacred by Saddam using chemical weapons. He drew this conclusion because Tony had not signed a particular EDM on the subject at the time. A ludicrous conclusion, which could only have been reached if one assumes that every MP sits down every day and goes meticulously through the published list of EDMs and signs every single one with which they agree.

Perhaps there are some MPs who do this, but very few. Most of us will sign EDMs where we've been asked to by constituents (provided we actually agree with them) and those motions in which we have a particular interest. But it would be nonsense to claim that the absence of a member's signature from an EDM will, on every occasion, suggest opposition.

The government: my part in its downfall
Published: February 24, 2009

The government lost a vote in the Commons today and I think it might have been my fault.

Let me explain…

I received a text message from the whips saying there was a vote expected. So I trooped into the chamber to see that the Lib Dem MP Susan Kramer was using the device of a ten-minute rule bill to push a silly idea about having Parliament approve every planning application by major airports. Bonkers, of course, but … well, she's a Lib Dem, what more can I say?

She was followed by David Wilshire, the Tory MP for Spelthorne and, on this subject at least, a good egg. He spoke for a few minutes on the general dottiness of Susan's proposal before sitting down.

Now, this is how ten-minute rule bills work: the member promoting it speaks for ten minutes and then, usually without a vote, it's agreed by the House, a date is set for Second Reading and it's never heard of again. However, this time, there *was* opposition. From me. Because when the Deputy Speaker asked those who opposed it to say 'No', I did. And when it looked as if she was unconvinced by the sincerity and volume of our protests and was going to give the day to Susan and her followers, I thought: 'No chance, let's have a vote – that'll show them!'

So I shouted louder, joined by a paltry few from our side and, of course, David Wilshire. Hearing the full strength of opposition to the measure, the Deputy Speaker had no choice. 'Division!' she announced, and I sped off to the 'No' lobby.

And then we lost. By more than thirty votes, I think. A couple of wags on the Lib Dem benches shouted 'Resign!' at me, before realising I was in no position to do so. I can't remember the government ever losing a vote on a ten-minute rule bill before. And now, following the vote, Susan's bill will … never be heard of again.

Would there have been a vote anyway, even if I hadn't shouted? Perhaps, but perhaps not. I fear I may be the guilty man, without whose intervention my government may well have avoided humiliation.

It seemed like a good idea at the time. There's a phrase that will be etched on my gravestone…

No blogging today

Published: February 25, 2009

Carolyn and I were genuinely saddened to hear the news that David and Samantha Cameron's son, Ivan, had died after a lifelong illness. I posted the following piece, and a number of readers left some very moving comments. I printed it out and sent it, comments included, to David, along with a brief note from me and Carolyn.

A small PS: Until this point, I had been running a fake Twitter account in David Cameron's name; it was supposed to be funny, with stuff like 'Took the children out to play in the snow and we all pelted the footman with snow until he bled. What larks!' But when Ivan died,

I received a number of sympathetic tweets from people who thought it was a genuine feed, so I deleted the account.

Having heard the terrible news about David Cameron's son, I don't think it would be appropriate to blog anything today.

It's at times like this that I realise how unimportant party politics can seem in comparison with life's important issues. I simply cannot imagine how David and Sam are feeling today and I know all our thoughts and prayers are with them.

But soft! What light through yonder window breaks? Oh, as you were – it's only Philip Davies
Published: February 27, 2009

Many a cup of Darjeeling would have been spat across the breakfast table at the homes of 'Outraged of Tunbridge Wells' this morning when news of the performance of *Romeo and Julian* was reported in (where else?) *The Telegraph*.

Philip Davies, a Conservative MP (who else?) raised the issue at Business Questions and was reportedly indignant at the prospect of these limp-wristed blighters seeking to convert innocent children to their perverted way of life, etc., etc.…

'Romeo and Julian' is a new version of the Shakespeare play, which is being performed in a handful of schools as part of Gay, Lesbian, Bisexual and Transgender Awareness Week. Inevitably, Philip Davies described this as 'political correctness', thereby damning it in the eyes of many.

Now, as you will know, I'm no fan of political correctness when it's taken to its silly extremes. But this is hardly an example of that. There's no doubt a lot of homophobic bullying goes on in schools and elsewhere and it's only right that children are made aware of why it happens and how to stop it. If *Othello* were re-written explicitly as an anti-racist tract, would Mr Davies also describe it as 'politically correct'?

I've no doubt that large numbers of people will respond to Davies's dog whistle as he intended. But to many others – particularly those who have gay or lesbian children – this initiative will be welcomed.

The Tories must accept the decision of the House
Published: June 16, 2009

I ended up voting for Parmjit Dhanda in the first ballot and Sir George Young in the subsequent ones.

Having used my podcast to declare publicly my support for John Bercow as the next Speaker, I'm delighted that, for the first time, some non-sectarian sense seems to have descended on at least one corner of the Tory blogosphere. Jonathan Isaby, an all-round good chap (for a Tory) has written a piece for *ConservativeHome* in support of Bercow's candidacy. This is in stark contrast to the party line taken so far by most online Tories.

Contrast Jonathan's thoughtful and sensible words with utter nonsense, also from *ConservativeHome*, where ~~brave~~ unnamed Tory MPs actually threaten to remove Bercow at the start of the next parliament if he's elected next week. This speaks volumes about David Cameron's Conservatives, but three things spring to mind:

1. After years of whining about Michael Martin's alleged sympathy towards his former party, it seems their main grievance was that they didn't have a Speaker biased towards *them*;
2. So much for the 'new politics' of the Cameron era within the Conservative Party – they're as cynical and partisan as they ever were; and
3. Today's Conservative Party believes the government party should decide who becomes Speaker.

There's been a lot of utter nonsense spoken and written about how Bercow's popularity among Labour MPs is all to do with a government whipping operation aimed at saddling a future Tory government with a Speaker they don't want. 'He'll be the third Labour Speaker in a row', according to one of the Great Anonymous Spineless, says *ConservativeHome*. I genuinely don't know of a single Labour MP worth his or her salt who would pay the slightest attention to the views of a government whip on this matter. I decided at the outset that I would support a Conservative MP. I then decided, independently, that if Bercow stood, I would support him. This is nothing to do with his level of support or popularity on his own benches. Choose to disbelieve me if you wish, but that will nevertheless remain a fact. Votes for the Speaker will be anonymous, so never again will a Speaker be able to be undermined in the way Michael Martin was, by grumbling and complaining that he was elected by the votes of the Labour Party. Bercow may indeed win thanks to Labour support, but we will never know for certain.

I offer two challenges to Bercow's detractors: if you believe there's a strong case for removing him for party political reasons after the next general election, then publicly explain what that case is without hiding behind anonymous briefings.

Secondly, whoever is elected Speaker will have my support, whether or not I voted for him or her. That's how democracy works; you express your view and then accept the result, even if you disagree with it. Will every Tory MP say likewise? Or will these spineless men of little principle continue to hide behind their anonymous briefings and plot to politicise the Speaker's office, thereby undermining the institution of the Commons itself?

Peeing with the enemy

Published: June 22, 2009

The Labour colleague in this next post was David Cairns. I can't remember now why he wanted to remain anonymous at the time. Shortly after this was published (and had been repeated by a number of the print media), David Cameron stopped me in the chamber during a vote and told me that conversations in Commons urinals should be considered unattributable and off the record. True, I replied. On the other hand, I hadn't been privy to the conversation – it had been reported by a third party. And anyway, the post had done Cameron no harm among his own colleagues.

Siobhan McDonagh later quoted the story during her eulogy for David Cairns at his memorial service in May 2011, in the presence of Mr Speaker himself.

A Labour colleague was in the toilet next to the chamber just before the first ballot, when he was joined by David Cameron in the adjacent urinal.

'David, I'm about to vote Tory for the very first time in my life,' said my friend jovially.

'John Bercow doesn't count!' replied Cameron.

Closer my God to thee

Published: July 7, 2009

I overheard a rather unkind reference to the denizens of the Upper House this evening:

> **Labour Lord:** *'We're voting on assisted dying tonight – putting old people out of their misery.'*
> **Labour MP:** *'Turkeys voting for Christmas, then?'*

In the end they didn't. Vote for Christmas, I mean.

New boy: Part 1

Published: July 19, 2009

As a general election approaches, my thoughts turn increasingly to the earlier, less complicated days of my political 'career'. A commenter in a previous thread suggested some readers may have some interest in my reminiscences of when I was first elected to the House. Don't know if that's true, but it's fun for me, if nobody else, to reflect.

I had never stood for any elected office before the 2001 general election. I had tried – and failed – to be selected as a Labour candidate in the 1990 regional council elections (and lessons learned at the time helped me win ten years later), so 2001 was the first time I had had to appoint an agent, attend the count as a candidate, stand on the platform, make an acceptance speech... The whole nine yards, as it were.

Before leaving home for the count, Carolyn and I ordered Chinese food for a number of key activists with whom we watched the early results and projections on TV before heading into the Scottish Exhibition and Conference Centre (SECC), where the Glasgow votes are counted. There had never been any real doubt that Labour would hang on for a second term or that our majority would be in three figures. Given an expected 160-seat margin between Labour and all the opposition parties combined, I didn't expect that we would lose Cathcart, and of course we didn't. But some of the more experienced activists had estimated my majority would fall to below 8,000 on a low turnout. In the end it was 10,816, or 39.5 per cent of the total vote, slightly up on the percentage majority I inherited from my predecessor, John Maxton.

Much to my surprise, my mum and dad insisted on attending the count and, since they were both in their sixties, I was concerned that they were unprepared for how long the night would last. But it meant a lot to me when my mum told me how proud she was when I made my acceptance speech as Cathcart's new MP. I didn't know at the time that she wouldn't live to see another general election.

Glasgow Cathcart was the last of the city's nine seats to be announced, so it was well after three by the time we were able to leave the SECC. Some hardier souls went on to other venues for more alcohol and more analysis, but Carolyn and I had had enough. We headed home. I woke up the next morning to various congratulatory telephone calls, including one from my (then) only son, who had enjoyed the excitement of the local campaign and had proudly worn a red rosette on which my name had been covered by a sticker saying simply: 'Vote Dad.'

Then there was a news conference and photo opportunity for all Scottish Labour's victorious candidates at our Scottish HQ in West Regent Street. After that, more R and R before heading to Castlemilk Labour Club that evening for an obligatory and traditional appearance as the new MP.

But after that, what? When should I head down to London? No one had been in touch to explain where and when to go, and in my exhaustion I hadn't actually asked any of my new colleagues when I met them at HQ on the Friday. I knew from media reports that the new parliament wouldn't meet until Wednesday 13 June. Is that when I should turn up? Or earlier?

Carolyn and I had decided that Tuesday would be a suitable date to head to London. Then Monday morning's mail arrived and it included a large, white, official-looking envelope with the legend 'From the Government Chief Whip' printed in the corner. Exciting stuff. It contained a lot of information giving answers to some of the questions I had. Importantly, it mentioned that advice surgeries for new Members were being held in the Commons from Monday onwards. Carolyn could see I was anxious to get down as early as possible. 'Just go today,' she told me. I was showered and heading for the airport within the hour.

Although Cathcart was a nominally 'safe' seat, I refused to book a hotel room in London until after I was elected, lest I tempt fate. Consequently, the only hotel I could get at short notice was a bit of a hovel in Belgrave Road, whose only advantage was that it was within walking distance of the House. Eagerly, I dumped my suitcase and began the walk up Millbank towards Westminster.

I was familiar with the House as a frequent visitor in my previous job, so I knew my best bet was to go to the St Stephen's entrance, where the public queue for access. I had been advised by John Maxton to bring with me some election leaflets with my face on it to distribute to the police officers and Serjeant-at-Arms staff to help them recognise me. This seemed sensible, but apart from the leaflets, how else could I prove who I was? Ever the pessimist, I envisaged a long, arduous conversation with the security guards, ending in my being refused entry pending my obtaining some form of official ID through a convoluted and circuitous route.

Hardly. I walked up to the first police officer I met and said: 'Excuse me, but I've just been elected and I—'

'Right this way, sir,' he replied before I'd even finished. He led me straight past the security barriers, past the metal detectors and up to Central Lobby where he handed me over to a member of the Serjeant-at-Arms staff who introduced himself as Michael and suggested the first thing I do was get my member's security pass. As he accompanied me through the rabbit warren of the palace to the desk where I would be photographed and issued with my pass, I asked him: 'Don't you need to check who I am?'

'No need for that, sir,' replied Michael.

'So, how do you know I really am an MP?'

After a slight pause, Michael opened a door and announced, 'Here we are, sir. Just take a seat.'

Five minutes later, I had my pass, and felt slightly less of an intruder. But only slightly, and the fact is, that feeling has never entirely dissipated in the last eight years.

New boy: Part 2

Published: July 26, 2009

New MPs don't get an office right away. Time was when they could spend a whole parliament or more without getting a space to themselves. But that was before Portcullis House was built. Unfortunately, newer members don't get anywhere near those plush, sunlit, state-of-the-art offices less than a minute's walk from the chamber. Nevertheless, the opening of Portcullis House did mean a lot of other offices were made available to the rest of us.

But we're getting ahead of ourselves. When I was first elected, for those first, frantic few weeks between polling day and the start of the long summer recess, I had to share a large room with at least half a dozen other new MPs. And it wasn't even a permanent arrangement, more of a hot-desk kind of thing. You would go to the members' Post Office in the morning to pick up your mail, which was handed over in either one or two green canvas hold-alls. Then you would make your way up to the room in the hope of securing a free desk and a telephone line, then sift through the mountains of mail.

Oh, how we laughed when, about a week in, we heard tell of a colleague, another new MP, who didn't realise he was supposed to collect his mail each day and who, after being told of the arrangement, had to recruit help in order to carry the ten green canvas bags full of mail up to the communal office, where he spent just about every waking hour for the next three days trying to wade through it.

As a new MP you inspect each item of correspondence closely. You also tend to accept as many invitations as possible. But you quickly learn to recognise those letters and invitations which aren't all that relevant and which should be consigned straight to the bin.

On the Wednesday after the election, the day the new House of Commons was to meet for the first time, I was going through my mail and looking for something specific. I had left home in such haste that I had neglected to take with me both my credit card and my cheque book, both of which I now needed. So I had asked Carolyn to post them, which she did, separately, for security reasons. When I found the empty, open envelopes I knew I was in trouble.

Both the card and the cheque book had been posted from St Vincent Street Post Office in Glasgow. And somewhere between there and the Commons, they had been nicked. Mobile phones costing hundreds of pounds had been charged to my card and my chequebook had been used to set up a standing order for a mobile phone contract. I discovered the theft barely minutes before the bell went for prayers, and rushed down to the chamber completely flustered and depressed. Not the best way to experience a packed chamber for the first time.

Then there was the Queen's Speech and the official opening of Parliament. And that means no votes. But that didn't mean that I and other new colleagues didn't want to be around the place and to make the most of our new work environment.

With a very few exceptions, the friends I made among the 2001 intake are friends I have stayed close to in the intervening years. Most MPs tend to bond more easily with colleagues of the same intake. Carolyn joined me in London for part of the rest of what was left of the summer term before recess, and my memories of that time are unfailingly happy: the weather was almost unbearably hot, there was an air of excitement (at least on the Labour benches), the Tories looked like they were about to refuse to elect Ken Clarke as leader, again. In other words, all was right with the world.

Recess was spent trying to get my constituency arrangements in place (this actually took much longer than I had anticipated and I was without a constituency office until the following March), trying to keep up with constituency cases, sorting out a schedule of surgeries and associated publicity material.

And then, on September 11, everything changed.

In the space of just a few hours, as I watched those awful scenes unfold on TV, my optimism turned to pessimism, international and domestic priorities were instantly transformed as our own understanding and assumptions about our world were challenged, shattered and reshaped.

My honeymoon as a new MP, like so many other things that day, had ended.

New boy: taking the oath

Published: October 5, 2009

Okay, so you've been selected as a candidate in a seat your party can reasonably expect to win at the election, you've been duly elected to serve your constituents and you've been given your security pass by the helpful staff at the House of Commons.

What next? The oath, of course.

In our last episode of this series, I recounted how I had only just discovered my credit card and cheque book had been nicked in the post, mere minutes before I was due to take my seat in the Commons for the very first time. Well, I managed to quell my feelings of anger and indignation towards the unidentified thief long enough to enjoy the business before the House that Wednesday afternoon. The first, and most important, item was the election of a Speaker. To preside over this, the Father of the House, Tam Dalyell, took a seat next to the clerks in front of the empty Speaker's chair and called for nominations. I can't now recall who proposed the Rt Hon. member for Glasgow Springburn, but I remember one was a Tory and the other Labour. No other nominations were forthcoming, and so, after a brief speech from Michael, he was duly 'dragged' to the chair.

He then announced that members wishing to take the oath should approach the chair. This is when, as a new member, you get an idea of your place in life. Privy councillors, cabinet members, shadow cabinet members and other ministers and frontbench spokespersons take priority. I was advised not to bother waiting, since there were approximately 600 people ahead of me in the queue. So I decided to wait until the following day.

The problem the next day was that I wanted to be back in my constituency for the first general committee of my local party since the election. To make it on time I would have to catch the 5.40pm flight from Heathrow and, after building in check-in, security and time to travel to the airport itself, I realised I would have to leave by about three at the latest. After waiting in line for a while, I realised I couldn't swear the oath and make it back to Glasgow on time. So I decided the oath could wait until the following week.

My biggest mistake was not postponing the oath-taking. No, no... My biggest mistake was buying new shoes.

Like most shoes I buy, they were slightly uncomfortable at first, but I knew all I had to do was wear them in. I might as well have taken a knife to my feet. I was in such pain after wearing them for the whole of Monday morning that I had to visit the nurse in the small room just off Lower Waiting, next to Central Lobby, to ask for help. One foot was in such a mess that she had to use a heavy duty bandage on it just to make it possible for me to walk. And not only did I have to walk that day – I had to stand in the queue of other members waiting to take the oath. For a very, very long time...

Slowly, I approached the clerk's table and the Speaker's chair. I had thought long and hard about whether I should take the religious oath or whether I should instead use the non-religious text to 'affirm' my loyalty to Queen Elizabeth and her heirs. At that time I hadn't been near a church for years and was still trying to work out where I was in relation to God and the church, so not wishing to appear a hypocrite, I chose to affirm. I held up my right hand, as instructed by the clerk, and, taking the card proffered by a man in a wig in my left hand, read out the words on the card.

Then, as I passed by the Speaker's chair, I was announced as the member for Glasgow Cathcart by another official, and Mr Speaker shook my hand and officially welcomed me to the Commons. There was no time for anything other than a cursory 'Thank you, Mr Speaker', since there was still a substantial queue behind me. I moved forward to the area behind the Speaker's chair and here

I was invited by yet another official to express a preference as to how my name should appear in Hansard, Parliament's official record, and on the 'annunciator' – the TV screens located throughout the palace which constantly announce the names of whichever speakers are currently addressing the Commons and the Lords. I chose 'Mr Harris' over 'Tom Harris'. Don't know why. I guess I was in a formal sort of mood at the time.

Then I signed my name and, at last, I was a Member of Parliament. Officially. Oh, and I would get paid now, which you can't until you've taken the oath.

It doesn't really matter that much when you take your first oath, unless you intend, one day, to become either Mother or Father of the House. And to do that you have to be elected very young and/ or serve for a ridiculously long period of time. For example, by the time Tam Dalyell became Father of the House, he had been an MP continuously for thirty-eight years. If you swore the oath on the same day as someone else elected for the first time on the same day as you, then in forty years' time, when you and he are vying for the honour of becoming Father of the House, whoever got sworn in first will win out.

When the Conservative MP Bernard Braine was in line to take the oath after the 1950 general election, he was ahead of another new boy, Ted Heath, in the queue. Thirty-seven years later, following the 1987 election, Sir Bernard was in line to become the new Father of the House. It is reported that he was approached by a very imperious Heath who suggested that, since Ted had served as the nation's Prime Minister and Sir Bernard … well, hadn't, then Sir Bernard may want to consider stepping aside in favour of Ted. Sir Bernard is reported to have offered Ted the kind of advice which former Prime Ministers rarely receive. Ted had to wait another five years, after Sir Bernard's retirement in 1992, to get his turn.

Poet's Corner
Published: October 15, 2009

Gordon Brown made an unintended (but rather good) attempt at stand-up poetry on Monday night as he addressed the Parliamentary Party:

> It has been a difficult time, a difficult day
> And difficult letters are on the way

So is this a new development in political communication, I wonder? At the risk of encouraging some unprintable attempts at similar rhymes from readers, may I suggest this for David Cameron:

> It's Gordon Brown, not me, who's failing
> I do hope someone's told Chris Grayling

Or how about this for Nick Clegg:

> Why can't everyone be as pure as me?
> The voters would thank, not moan at us
> Yes they're less honest than I
> But I'm going home to cry
> Cos I can't find a rhyme for 'sanctimonious'

Okay, folks – do your worst. But please remember, this is a family blog.

Happy birthday, Ipsa!
Published: August 3, 2010

The Independent Parliamentary Standards Authority (Ipsa) has become the bane of every MP's life since the 2010 general election. 'And quite right too!' I hear you splutter. Well, maybe. But the fact is that the incompetence and lack of foresight which ministers brought to its unhappy birth has been more than matched by its own incompetence and inability to understand what MPs need to be able to run their office, or even what MPs are for. There now follow a couple of posts, selected from many I could have included here.

Ipsa have embarked on a charm offensive to mark its three-month anniversary.

Now, you should know that both Ian Kennedy, Ipsa's chair, and its chief executive, Andrew McDonald, are very touchy and a tad hysterical when it comes to criticism. Kennedy told *The Telegraph* just last month that 'All of these are claims that have rained down on us, all made with gusto – and every one untrue.'

So, the chairman of Ipsa believes every MP who has made a complaint about Ipsa – including all of us who took part in a Westminster Hall debate on the subject on 16 June – is a liar. Interesting... (I wrote to Mr Kennedy today, inviting him to place on record his belief that I am lying in my criticisms of Ipsa but I expect he won't reply – I'm only an MP, after all, not a journalist.)

Now Andrew McDonald is patting himself on the back because, three months after it was up and running, Ipsa have managed to pay his and Mr Kennedy's salaries on time and in full. So, job done.

McDonald, responding to outrageous and unfounded claims that the Ipsa computer system is crap, said:

'MPs' offices spend around fifteen minutes a day doing their online expenses – which, given the significant sums of public money involved, does not seem unreasonable – and we now settle claims within thirteen days.'

I'm sure his Director of Corporate Information and Communications Technology, or one of his three deputy directors, told McDonald that this was the case. But how does he know that on each occasion, the person using the system logged off entirely happy with the service? Yesterday, for example, I gritted my teeth and logged on to try to make some claims. As per procedure, after a few minutes I tried to phone Ipsa to ask for help. I waited for fifteen minutes before hanging up and trying again. Then the phone cut out on me after I'd got through. Then I tried again and it was engaged. I tried three more times and on the third time I got through to a very helpful gentleman who explained how I could progress my session. He rung off and I continued my session. Then discovered I was locked out of the system. I gave up.

Now, in IpsaLand, this was simply an MP logging onto the system and then, half an hour or so later, logging out. But on planet Earth, this was an MP giving up in frustration and not claiming money that was due to him. I get the feeling that that's the point of the system.

As for claims being paid within thirteen days, the only claims that I know of that are paid that quickly are mileage claims. Many colleagues have claimed bitterly that they are thousands of pounds out of pocket thanks to Ipsa's tardiness. But then, they're MPs and are therefore lying, according to Mr Kennedy.

McDonald continues:

'All I will say is that I am pleased with what we have achieved to date – against daunting odds.'

Daunting odds? Ah, yes – the outrageously difficult task of paying 650 people identical salaries and paying out expenses. A feat no organisation has ever dared attempt before now.

Ominously – and you can almost hear the threat in his voice as you read it – McDonald tells *The Telegraph*:

'...in 2011/12 we will undertake our first review of MPs' pay. To have an informed – public – discussion of pay, we need to ask fundamental questions about the role of MPs and what they need from the taxpayer to perform that role.'

Oh, well, that's going to work out well, isn't it? 'So, tell me, Mr Average Member of the Public, do you think that overpaid MPs – remember, the ones who stole all that money from you over the years and spent it on duck houses and such? – should get even more money?'

His boss, Ian Kennedy, recently made a speech in which he claimed:

'It is one of the peculiar ironies of fate that MPs voted en masse for the creation of Ipsa, only for some, the refuseniks, to expend a great deal of energy criticising it and its staff.'

That's not how I remember it, matey-boy. Yes, there were some votes on some of the dafter things that Jack Straw inserted into the Bill on stuff like parliamentary privilege, but there was no vote on the Second or (I think) the Third Reading. This was not because, as Kennedy no doubt tells himself as he's crying himself to sleep at night, everyone enthusiastically supported the legislation; it was because we made the colossal mistake of considering the legislation in the midst of the expenses scandal – the worst possible time to give due consideration to such an important Bill. No one in their right minds would have spoken out against its measures given the rapidity with which the media would have leapt on them, destroying with self-righteous relish any chance of re-election for that individual.

No, there's never been a vote on Ipsa in the past. But there might be one soon. And I suspect we'll be a lot less reticent this time about expressing our views in the lobbies.

They've got forms
Published: August 9, 2010

What most people forget about MPs' expenses was the year between the scandal and the general election.

During that year the House of Commons fees office processed all claims and published them online. Every penny was accounted for. There was no fiddling, it was completely transparent and the whole thing was undertaken for about two million quid.

Oh, happy days… I remember them well. I often regale newbie MPs with stories about the old expenses system and they listen, wide-eyed and incredulous. 'So they would actually pay you money that you'd claimed?' they gasp over their tea, awestruck, eyes glistening as their minds try to comprehend such a blessed utopia.

'And they would, like, *believe* you if you said you had children? I mean, they didn't insist that you provide their birth certificates to prove that you hadn't invented them in order to buy children's rail tickets on the public purse and then sell them on the black market?'

The look of shock is tinged with grudging admiration and I smile gently as I stir my tea. 'Nope,' I reply. 'Hard to believe now, but in them days we didn't have to prove we had families. If we had just made them up, some snooping reporter would probably have exposed us anyway.'

'I heard a rumour that back in the Olden Days, the Fees Office would pay bills direct to the supplier!' says one excited young MP from somewhere Oop North. 'Is that true? Tell us, Tom, do tell us!'

I nod sagely and pretend to light up a pipe, but I look stupid so quickly place the imaginary pipe back in my pocket. 'Indeed, young Andrew...'

'Mike.'

'Indeed, young Mike, there was a time when we would receive bills and we would simply authorise them with a signature and pass them on to the Fees Office, which would take care of them for us.'

'But what on earth did you do with all your time, then? If it only took you a few minutes a month to claim expenses? Didn't you get bored without the need to spend all day on a computer yelling and crying?'

'Well, in those days we would actually use our time to help constituents!'

There is an audible collective gasp, and silence falls. I use the temporary gap to play my trump card: 'And do you know how many forms we had to fill in?' There is some confusion on the young faces as they anxiously start counting fingers. One woman starts using the calculator on her mobile phone. 'Three!' I declare, and the silence this time is deafening...

It's true − that bit about the forms. There was a green one for mileage, a yellow one for your second home allowances and a blue one for office costs. No wonder it was an efficient system. You'd list however many items on each form, sign it, attach the necessary receipts, shove it in the nearest post box and hey presto – a few days later you'd have it paid into your account (or paid direct to suppliers) and you'd get a separate notification through the post listing the details of everything you'd claimed and everything that had been paid out.

Now, to Ipsa...

This is the list of forms you get to choose from when you log on:

Expense Claims and Registration
Expenses: Accommodation
Expenses: Conts. Rent
Expenses: General Admin
Expenses: Interim Accomm.
Expenses: Mileage
Expenses: Miscellaneous
Expenses: Staffing
Expenses: Travel Foreign Curr.
Expenses: Travel/Subsist.
Expenses: Winding Up
Income: Subletting
Loan: Request for loan
Receipts: Supporting invoice
Registration: Accomm. Status
Registration: Const. Office
Registration: Dependant
Registration: Disability
Registration: Init Declaration
Registration: Security Need
Registration: Vehicle

Then, once you've chosen a category, you're presented with a drop-down menu of all the different options again. Then, on top of that, you have to write in your own description of whatever your claim is.

'Tell us the colours again, Tom. Please. They sound so pretty...' But I've indulged my audience for long enough. It's nearly six o'clock and the House rises at ten, so I don't have long to submit my own claims. I depart, leaving the young parliamentarians staring into space, dreaming of blue skies and green trees and fields of yellow corn as far as the eye can see…

All political careers end in failure, some earlier than others…

Published: October 10, 2010

To be fair to Ed Miliband, he invited me for a chat in his office after the dust had settled on the reshuffle and expressed regret at not knowing I had been keen to return to the front bench. A few weeks later he kept his promise to bear me in mind in future by offering me a frontbench post that had fallen unexpectedly vacant. I turned him down.

So that was my career, was it? A minister for barely two years – appointed by Blair, sacked by Brown, left on the backbenches by Miliband.

Not exactly the material for a best-selling political diary, but that's politics for you. Nobody ever said life was fair.

I entertained the hope, for a while, that I might yet have a contribution to make towards the success of my party. Apparently not.

Some good people have been promoted to the front bench, though, and I wish them well, albeit through gritted teeth…

Career killers

Heaven knows we're miserable now
Published: June 19, 2008

The media broo-haha over the 'Heaven knows we're miserable now' post was only so intense because I was a minister at the time. I'm not aware of any actual fallout as regards my career; the only reaction I got from my immediate bosses was from Ruth Kelly, then Transport Secretary, who very kindly asked me if I was okay.

I say there was no fallout – not quite true. As a result of my newfound notoriety, I was asked to appear on BBC's Question Time *a couple of weeks later. Three days away from filming and I received a phone call from a friend who worked at Number 10, asking me to withdraw. I was gutted, and said no, and anyway, I had already blogged that same morning that I was to appear on the panel. I hung up and waited on the next inevitable phone call from someone higher up the food chain. When it came, it was from another friend (and no, I didn't have lots of friends at Number 10 while Gordon was PM; I had two). How would I be able to respond when Nicola Sturgeon, the SNP deputy leader and another member of that week's panel, challenged me about why people are unhappy? Especially sensitive, given the upcoming by-election in Glasgow East. 'I think I can handle her,' I responded. And given that I'd spent forty-eight hours answering every possible combination of questions about the post from every part of the media, I think I could say so with a degree of confidence. But the decision had been taken. The game was up. Resignedly, and utterly devastated, I told my friend he could give whatever excuse they wanted to the Beeb. In my place they got David Cairns, who felt guilty about replacing me. Shortly after appearing, David resigned over Gordon's leadership. And we lost the Glasgow East by-election anyway.*

I've been listening to the audiobook of Bill Bryson's excellent *The Life and Times of the Thunderbolt Kid*, his autobiographical account of his early life in Iowa.

It's as funny, charming and wistful as you would expect, full of fantastic imagery of post-World War II consumerism, invention and prosperity. And, of course, it harks back to the innocence of a childhood utopia that probably didn't actually exist.

But what struck me with the most force was the sheer optimism of the time. Even with the constant threat of nuclear obliteration, with memories of the war still vivid in most adults' heads, most US citizens seemed to believe the future was brighter than the past. Their country was the wealthiest, the most powerful and, yes, the happiest on the face of the planet. National leaders were respected and even liked (as in Ike). In a pre-Watergate era, politicians, though viewed through a healthy filter of cynicism, were nevertheless acknowledged as local and national leaders, essential to the workings of a democracy that, having been fought for only recently, was still precious.

So where did it all go wrong? In our own country today, despite the recent credit squeeze, our citizens have never been so wealthy. High-def TVs fly off the shelves at Tesco quicker than they can be imported. Whatever the latest technological innovation, most people can treat themselves to it. Eating out – a rare treat when I was a child in the 1970s – is as commonplace as going shopping. And when we do go shopping, whether for groceries or for clothes, we spend money in quantities that would have made our parents gasp.

We're securer than ever, at least in international terms. There's no equivalent of the Soviet Union threatening to bury us in a nuclear armageddon. The very real threat of terrorism hasn't notably altered anyone's patterns of behaviour or travel (which is as it should be). Job security is felt to be less than in the past, it's true, but the corollary of that is the tremendous real-terms rises in incomes over the years and the consequent improvements in quality of life.

There are more two-car homes in Britain today than there are homes without a car at all. We live longer, eat healthier (if we choose), have better access to forms of entertainment never imagined a generation ago (satellite TV, DVD, computer games), the majority of us have fast access to the worldwide web, which we use to enable even more spending and for entertainment. Crime is down.

So why is everyone so bloody miserable?

Are our crippling levels of cynicism and pessimism simply part of the human condition? Were we always like this? Or is a consequence of the 'instant gratification society' that, having been instantly gratified, we must resent the society that manipulates our desires in this way?

I will, on this one occasion, concede that the mass media can't be held entirely to blame, just as I hope readers of this blog will accept that our elected leaders are similarly not 100 per cent guilty.

But what happened to that post-war optimism and commitment to common values? Are they gone forever and if so, why? If not, how can we bring them back?

Heavy stuff, I know, but occasionally you want to talk about more than the latest episode of *Doctor Who*.

The return of morality
Published: March 4, 2009

And so to my 'tirade' against teenage parents. Some of the valid criticism made of this post was my over-emphasis on girls rather than boys. But the gist of the piece was and remains correct; a lot of comfortable middle-class commenters are very happy with the notion of young working-class people becoming parents before they've become adults – provided it doesn't happen to their own children.

When Carolyn was in hospital, having just delivered us of wee Reggie, a very young girl in the bed opposite was also celebrating the arrival of her newborn. As was her father, who made great play to anyone who might have been listening (me) of how proud he was of his daughter. She was, I guess, about sixteen.

I don't think he should have been ashamed. And it's great that this young girl had such a loving dad to support her.

But proud? Proud that his teenage daughter was not only sexually active but was now a mother? Proud that any chance of a decent education, followed by a decent job, was now remote at best? Proud that she was, in all likelihood, about to embark on a lifetime of depending on benefit handouts for her and her child?

I'm a Labour MP, so some will undoubtedly be surprised and shocked that I'm writing this. But I can no longer pretend that the army of teenage mothers living off the state is anything other than a national catastrophe.

A previous commenter on this site got it spot on: many (though not all) teenage girls do not become pregnant accidentally because of ignorance, because of a lack of understanding of how their bodies work. They become pregnant because they have absolutely no ambition for themselves. They have been indoctrinated with the lie that they'll never amount to anything, and have fulfilled that prophecy by making no effort to achieve any qualification. Very often they live with parents (or a parent) who have no jobs themselves, who are setting the example of benefit dependency for all their offspring.

Such young women see parenthood as one way of achieving a level of independence and self-worth. And they're right, because that's more or less what they get: a flat and therefore some privacy, an income for the first time in their lives. And, in fact, many of them make a decent job of parenthood despite the awful circumstances. But even they are nevertheless rearing the next generation in an environment where the main adult isn't working, but claiming.

I was lucky. I was brought up in a relatively poor household, but both my parents worked for most of the time I was growing up. When my dad was out of work in the early 1980s, he was depressed because he felt a responsibility to earn money to provide for his family. And so he started up his own business and got back on his feet. That's the example I and my brothers and sister were lucky enough to have set for us.

A few years back I was shopping for CDs in Tower Records in Glasgow of a Saturday evening. It must have been about ten at night. Outside there were two very young girls, about fifteen, all dressed up for a night out. Apart from the fact that wherever they intended to go, they were clearly too young to drink, there was only one problem: one of them was pushing a pram. The child inside was a few weeks old.

This horrified me. It was wrong. There is right and wrong and it is wrong for anyone to choose to have a child without knowing what's involved in its upbringing, without being prepared to sacrifice your own lifestyle for it.

That father in the maternity ward was telling the world about his love for his daughter and his new grandchild, and I've no doubt his pride was genuine. People shouldn't be ashamed of their circumstances, but neither should we avoid making value judgments about others' choices, especially when those choices result in a greater burden on the state, and lead to the continuation of the underclass.

Teenage girls shouldn't be having underage sex. Why? Because it's wrong.

Teenage girls shouldn't choose to have babies as an alternative to getting an education and a career. Why? Because it's wrong.

Parents shouldn't teach their children that a lifetime on benefits is attractive or even acceptable. Why? Because it's wrong.

(Please assume all the usual caveats: some people have no choice but to claim benefits, lots of single parents do a great job, etc.)

So what's next, I hear you ask. What am I going to do about all this? What's the government going to do?

This post isn't about policy, yet. I'm going to take up a previous commenter's suggestion that I have a coffee with the estimable Frank Field to discuss ideas for reform.

But policies are one thing; winning the argument about why they're needed is another. And we have to start by making it clear what we believe is right and wrong. How can we expect parents to teach that to their kids if our political leaders aren't prepared to say the same?

Being accused of agreeing with the *Daily Mail*'s agenda is not the worst thing my critics can say about me. Being accused of accepting the current appalling state of affairs, of pretending that the concepts of right and wrong are meaningless – *that* is far worse than being accused of pandering to the right.

And, of course, it is a complete load of bollocks to suggest that the ordinary working-class people of Glasgow South and in hundreds of other constituencies throughout the country don't agree with me. The most vociferous critics of the dependency culture and of deliberate worklessness have always been those who live in the same communities, those who resent paying their taxes to help other people waste their lives.

Don't interpret this as any kind of 'back to basics' crusade; I'm not remotely interested in what adults do in the privacy of their own homes, and I'm not sounding the rallying cry for Christian or religious morality. But when the actions of others has such a debilitating effect on the rest of society, it's time to stop being polite. It's time to stop worrying about how people's feelings might be hurt if we question the choices they've made.

Because very often, those choices are wrong. And it's about time we said so.

Kind regards

Published: March 9, 2009

Among the generally positive responses to my previous interventions in the 'benefit dependency' and single mums debate, was a comment from 'Bill', a Labour councillor and a social worker.

It was a very full and thoughtful comment, and I wanted to take some time to respond to the points Bill made:

> I'm a Labour councillor, and I work as a social worker, tasked with safeguarding the most vulnerable children of all. I realise that you use this blog to express your 'anger'

about things quite a lot (teenage parents, child abuse) but I'm not sure being angry changes much or helps anybody. It doesn't in the job I do, for sure. Reasoned arguments and evidence might.

It would be nice if you spelt out a little more what exactly the hoped for outcome of your piece was? Have you achieved it? When and how will you know if you've been successful in your endeavours?

The hoped-for outcome of my piece is to start to achieve a change of mindset in the Labour Party and beyond, so that we can stop feeling obliged to pretend that every lifestyle choice people make is beyond criticism, even as the vast majority of the public, at least privately, have no qualms about such judgements. I believe such frankness would help Labour engage with the public more successfully.

Reading your post, I don't think it would help anyone if I responded to your post with personal attacks of any kind, although that's not consideration you seem to have thought to extend to the 'teenage mum' you refer to in your post.

Fortunately, I have never attacked any teenage mums in any of my writing, unless questioning the wisdom of someone's choice is strictly 'attacking'.

I did wonder a couple of things about your original post:

i) why don't you refer to boys/men – in their teenage years or older. I do wonder why the object of your onslaught falls exclusively on women rather than men. There's young fathers out there who do a brilliant job, yet there are many who aren't involved in their children's lives at all, for a variety of complex reason. I do wonder why you have attacked the girls/women literally left 'holding the baby', but leave the male sex entirely out of the equation. You do attack men in the *Mail on Sunday* (and I think attack is sadly the right word). Is this because you realised you had made a mistake is singling out just one, particularly vulnerable, group from criticism?

I don't feel the need, in my blog or elsewhere, to insert caveats which any intelligent reader would assume anyway. The point I made in my original post was about the economics of single parenthood; given the number of young single women who are subsidised by the state to care for their babies compared with the number of young single men, I didn't believe it was strictly relevant to include men in this part of the argument. I don't think the lack of mention of men's/boys' role in any way made the article less easy to understand.

In fact, the YWCA site, to which I was directed by another angry commenter, states:

> It needs to be better recognised and understood that young women who see little hope for their future are most likely to view early motherhood as a positive change to their lives. For young women with low self-esteem, tough lives, low incomes, low educational achievement and low aspirations, motherhood can provide a more prestigious and fulfilling status than the one they currently occupy.

Perhaps you should complain also to the YWCA about their lack of mention of the fathers.

> ii) you seem a little confused about age, Tom. Do you really think that the issues faced by 14-year-old mother and a 19-year-old mother, or their young children, might be subtly different? Can you think of any differences

here? It might be worth including them in any future articles.

I'm not at all confused about age, and I doubt if many of my readers, aside from you, of course, would have tripped up on that one.

iii) How many teenage mothers have you spoken to in preparation for your little piece? I do understand that you overhead a new baby's grandfather talking in hospital a while ago, but has your personal experience of this issue gone beyond that? I'm sure it has, but I do wonder why you don't seem to mention it.

This gets to the nub of the issue. I'm sure you are exempt here, but I have detected a degree of exclusiveness among professionals working in this area: 'We are the qualified professionals who work every day in this area with our "clients" and therefore we have an exclusive right to pontificate about what the issues are.' It could be almost interpreted as a closed shop situation. It's an unusual position to take: that an MP, whose job is to scrutinise legislation and to debate and decide how the nation's resources are spent, should not be able to express a view about a controversial area of public policy.

And in fact, in the course of eight years representing a constituency with one of the highest levels of teenage parenthood, I have spoken to many women of various ages about their experiences and circumstances.

iv) Given you have been a government minister, and represent a party which has been in office for nearly twelve years and doubtless you will represent a large number of young parents in Glasgow, don't you think it might have been a good idea to include any qualitative or quantitative evidence to support your arguments, other than a single anecdote, in your piece? I wonder if it might have been an idea to talk about some of the significant changes in Children's Services legislation and policy which I presume you have voted for, as they're clearly of relevance to this issue. Have you read, or even heard of, the Teenage Pregnancy Strategy (at a local or national level)? Don't you think it might have been a good idea to read it first?

Indeed, I'm well aware of the government's (and local authorities') Teenage Pregnancy Strategy and of the targets to reduce this problem by 2010. The problem, Bill, is that too many professionals – including you, I suspect – refuse to describe this problem as a 'problem'.

iv) I'm sure I'm not the only person to be saddened to read a Labour MP writing in the *Mail on Sunday* that Iain Duncan Smith, has a 'lot to offer' this area of debate. What precisely is that Tom, please explain? He didn't really have that much to offer his own party, and seeking to rebuild his career on his 'Broken Britain' hypothesis hasn't changed matters.

I happen to have been impressed by IDS's efforts at least to understand the problem, which is more than most in his party have done. I believe the issue of teenage pregnancy and the wider area of benefit dependency is so serious, so colossal, that no single party is going to be able to resolve it.

v) Just out of interest, why did you write this piece at this particular time? Did something happen to make you so very angry that you didn't want to write about? [sic] Just out of interest, don't you think it might be a little harder for the young parents to represent to find work now, compared to a year or two ago? I wonder if you thought this was worth mentioning?

Yes, the appalling death of 23-month-old Dundee toddler, Brandon Muir. A drug-addicted prostitute with learning difficulties was allowed to look after her young son because there aren't enough people around to stand up and say: 'That is grotesque.' Because the main point of my original post was not about teenage mums *per se*; it was about challenging the refusal of society publicly to judge others' lifestyle choices. I didn't mention Brandon's case specifically because there's no direct correlation and I could well imagine the howls of indignation: 'Tom Harris believes every single mother is unfit to look after her child!' Which, of course is nonsense. But the reports of Brandon's death and the subsequent court case started me thinking about the 'rights' of parents and how they should never take precedence over the rights of children to a loving and secure environment. And, following on from what the YWCA site (above) says, a child should never, ever be used as a way of achieving financial benefit for his parent.

> vi) Have you ever met personally, or directly heard about, any individual young woman who became pregnant purely and simply because of the benefit/housing entitlement this would create? Do you actually know of a single one? If so, and I think your answer may in any event be no, how are you sure that this was the case?

You're absolutely right on this one, Bill: the answer's no. In fact I'm far too polite to ask any woman of whatever age and background what her motivations were for becoming pregnant. But I refer you, again, to the YWCA site. It says almost exactly what I said in my previous post, although I did not come across the YWCA site until after I'd written it. Let me turn the question around: do you believe that there has never been a case of a young woman who felt her opportunities were so limited, her future so constrained, that she genuinely believed her best hope was to become a mother?

There is a clear correlation between poverty and the incidence of teenage pregnancy; NHS Scotland point out that women living in the worse off parts of the country are up to ten times more likely to fall pregnant at an early age than those living in wealthier areas. This seems to me conclusive evidence that poverty of aspiration and lack of education lies behind many such pregnancies.

Maybe I'm wrong, maybe the YWCA is wrong, maybe the NHS is wrong, maybe everyone who believes this is wrong. The fact that you've challenged me in my assumptions suggests you think they are. In which case, there's no problem, is there? Perhaps I shouldn't waste my time worrying about those young girls brought up in workless households by single parents and who achieve very little at school. Perhaps there is, after all, no such thing as poverty of aspiration.

But, of course, there is.

> I would be interested in your thoughts.
> Kind regards,
> Bill

You now have them, Bill.
> Kind regards
> Tom

September 2006:
the coup against Tony Blair

I had constituency surgeries on Friday 1 September 2006, both of which I was covering without the help of my long-time, loyal and very efficient researcher, Donald, who was on annual leave. I had some time to kill between meetings and I decided to spend a pleasant fifteen minutes at a cafe in a local church. When I re-emerged and prepared to drive to my next surgery, Chris Bryant phoned me.

I first met Chris when we both worked for the party back in 1991. He came up to the north east of Scotland to help out in the Kincardine and Deeside by-election, where Labour were fighting a valiant but vain campaign in a straight fight between the Tories and the Lib Dems. Within a few days of the 2001 general election, which brought us both to Westminster, (he had been elected for the ultra-safe Welsh seat of Rhonda) we met up again and became close friends.

I was taken aback by the content of this call, and wasn't entirely sure, at first, if Chris was being entirely serious. But he was: would I be prepared to add my name to a letter calling on Tony Blair to resign as Prime Minister and Labour leader?

At this time, I should explain, I was a member of the Ranks of the Disappointed Loyal. There used to be an assumption at Westminster that promotion to the front bench was not conferred or earned until you had served as a backbencher for at least a few years. After the accession of Miliband the Younger to the Labour leadership, that changed: quite a few newly-elected MPs have had to give up their paper rounds in order to assume frontbench responsibilities. But in government, unless you were part of the Assisted Places Scheme (in other words, served previously as a special adviser, or 'SPAD', in government for a cabinet minister or even the PM himself), you had to do your time learning the ropes both at Westminster and in your constituency before having power thrust upon you.

Some of us were made Parliamentary Private Secretaries in Blair's first reshuffle after the Iraq invasion (I was appointed PPS to the then Minister of State at Northern Ireland, John Spellar. Top bloke). But it was the reshuffle Blair embarked upon following his third successive general election victory in May 2005 on which the ambitious members of the 2001 intake of Labour MPs were focused.

For me, the call didn't come, and I found it hard to hide my disappointment. I was later called in for a chat with the Prime Minister in his House of Commons office and assured by Tony that he would find a space for me in a future reshuffle. Your time will come, he assured me. In the meantime, he was glad I had accepted the position of PPS to the new health secretary, Patricia Hewitt.

Then the reshuffle of May 2006 arrived. Still no call. As it happens, I had other things on my mind, with Carolyn only a few days away from giving birth to our second son. Nevertheless, the disappointment was keenly felt. My political career was passing before my very eyes, colleagues elected only a year earlier were now above me on the greasy poll.

I was not a happy camper and the party leadership knew it. Hazel Blears, the new party chair, was despatched to soothe the savage breasts of me and a few others who felt left out. We were offered the dizzy heights of party vice-chairs, which carried no responsibility, no prestige, no influence and certainly no salaries. I informed Hazel, who I like personally, that I would not accept these 'scraps from the table'.

By the time Reggie was born in June 2006, I was very contented. Although I wasn't happy with the way my 'career' had turned out, I had come to terms with being a permanent resident of the backbenches. Yes, I was angry at what I perceived as Tony's lack of good faith, but I reminded myself that even as a backbencher, I was in a very privileged position; there were plenty of people out there who would gladly have switched places with me.

That summer recess, I concentrated on enjoying my small and growing family. I also took the first tentative steps towards starting a blog – a medium with which I was becoming fascinated but which I knew almost nothing about. The first few columns were just that – opinion pieces written on my parliamentary website without any ability for readers (either of them) to leave comments or interact in any way.

But back to that first day of September, 2006...

Had I heard Chris correctly? He wanted to ask Tony to resign?

Many others from the 2001 intake had already agreed to sign. Chris, Tom Watson, the West Bromwich MP and a defence minister at the time, and Sion Simon, the Birmingham Edgbaston MP, seemed to be organising this round robin.

Is it a letter to the press? I asked.

No, it's a private letter to Tony.

But it will leak pretty quickly, I told him.

It won't leak, said Chris.

Hmm.

So would I sign?

Of course not. He did realise it was going to leak?

It won't leak.

*

That evening, as Carolyn and I sat watching TV, Chris rang again. Had I changed my mind about signing the letter?

Why on earth would I have?

More to the point, why was he so keen to add my name? Safety in numbers, I expect. But the more people privy to its contents and purpose, the more likely it was to leak. And the more difficult it would be to trace the source of the leak.

And so began my small part in the continuing farce of the TB-GB feud that had already caused so much harm to my party. Up until this point, I was considered something of a Brownite, if only because I was Scottish and I had made clear my view that, whenever Tony chose to leave of his own free will and at a time of his own choosing, I would support Gordon as successor. But I was totally against forcing Tony out before he was ready. Everyone knew he had to step down *during the 2005 parliament – he had already said as much. So what was the point in pushing a man who was already determined to jump?*

For what it's worth, even though I was prepared to support Gordon up until this point, I never believed he had any justification for resenting Tony for becoming leader in 1994, following John Smith's death. I remain firmly of the view that if GB had stood against Tony at the time, he would have lost and would have become a member of the shadow Cabinet on exactly the same terms as every other member, without Tony having to make any 'deals' about when he might step down. Ah, if only...

Pretty soon that weekend, the machinations of colleagues faded into irrelevance: during a visit to relatives in Perth on the Saturday, Reggie, still only three months old, developed a sinister-looking rash. After he was examined by a local doctor, we were told to take him to the children's hospital at Yorkhill, Glasgow, where we spent the most hellish night of our lives. Not as hellish as it was for poor wee Reggie, however, who had to undergo a lumber puncture so that his spinal fluid could be tested for the presence of meningitis.

Carolyn refused to leave his side that night, and stayed at the hospital while I returned to an empty, depressing house. Reggie's older brother, Ronnie, was staying with his grandmother.

And still the texts and phone messages were coming in. Whenever I switched my phone back on after leaving the ward, there would be new pleas for support from the conspirators. At one point Carolyn even asked me why I wasn't signing, since I had a legitimate greivance. The fact was I wished to remain loyal to the man whose political vision and skill had delivered three general election victories in a row, even if he hadn't given me a job.

On the Sunday evening, as I was preparing to leave the house and go back to the hospital, I received a call from Dave Wright, the amiable Telford MP and another of the signatories. He wanted to know if I could let him have Chris's number.

'Do you have a copy of the letter you've added your name to?' I asked.

'No,' he replied.

'Well, not to worry – I'll buy a Guardian *tomorrow and read it there.'*
Dave laughed. 'It's not going to leak, mate.'

*

Back in the children's hospital, wee Reggie was showing tentative signs of recovery, although he still had various tubes coming out of him. On the Monday he smiled at me for the first time in days and I told Carolyn I was sure this was a sign he was on the mend. I was right.

The tests had proved negative for meningitis, thank God, and positive for something called enterovirus. He would soon forget the pain and discomfort of those few days; we never will.

We had been told that, provided there were no more complications, Reggie could come home with us on Tuesday. As I drove to the hospital in Glasgow's west end to pick him and Carolyn up, the hands-free unit in my car indicated an incoming call. It was a friend who was also a reporter for The Guardian. *Was I aware of a letter signed by MPs from my intake calling for Tony Blair to resign?*

One of the reasons I have reasonably good relations with journalists is that I don't lie to them. I occasionally equivocate or exaggerate, but I don't lie. That morning, and to that journalist, I lied. What other option was there? I had no idea how much information the media had. If they had simply heard a rumour, I didn't want to be the one who confirmed it. The stakes were far too high and I wasn't going to make it easier for them to make Tony's – and the government's – life more difficult.

I also didn't want to start explaining why I had not signed the letter; maybe we could escape this particular row without yet another examination of the fraught relationship between the PM and his Chancellor.

Fortunately, I had to switch my morning phone off when I went back into the hospital to collect Reggie and his mum. I had some constituency visits to fulfill in the afternoon and during one of them, I was called by John McTernan at Number 10. Had I been asked to sign the letter? Would I be willing to sign a new letter, this time in support of Tony? My answer, of course, was yes, but I had some reservations about getting into a situation where support and opposition could be recorded in black and white according to the number of signatures each camp had.

The rest of the day was spent focusing on the family, rather than on less important political matters.

Wednesday morning's rolling news coverage was all about the 'attempted coup', as slavering journalists were calling it. Oh, and by the way – did I mention that the letter leaked? Who could've seen that coming?

Carolyn was just about to leave the house to pop up to the local Asda and would take Ronnie with her, leaving me to look after Reggie, who was now well on the way to recovery but who we still didn't want to take out of the house. As she left, we heard the report that Tom Watson, unsurprisingly, had resigned from the government because of his role in the coup.

'Hey, maybe I'll get the call this time,' I joked to her as she left.

Her smile said it for both of us: it's not going to happen, and that's fine. And I knew she was right.

I sat on the sofa, Reggie on my lap, cooing and gurgling at me. And I vividly recall thinking: this is what's important. He could have died and he didn't and he's healthy and thank God. Nothing else mattered.

But I was still a Labour MP and I still had a job to do. And today that job was offering whatever moral support I could to the PM. The phone was still ringing off the hook with journalists eager to talk to me about the past few days' events. I suspect the signatories' phones were even busier. No, I didn't think Tony should be forced out, yes he should resign at some point, as he had undertaken to do in 2004 and many times since, but the timing should be a matter for him.

Reggie didn't seem to mind the constant ringing and conversations I was having; he was back to being hs contented wee self. Then a stern, female voice on the other end of the line said: 'Is that Tom Harris?'

'Yes?'

'This is the switchboard at Number 10. Please hold for the Prime Minister.'

I wrote down the details of the call shortly afterwards. In essence, Tony thanked me for my support: 'I know you've come under a lot of pressure to add your name, and I appreciate your support.' Tom's resignation had created a vacancy at Defence, which was being filled by the transport minister, Derek Twigg. Tony wanted me to take Derek's place as railways minister. The Transport Secretary, Douglas Alexander, would be in touch shortly to discuss my duties, as would my new Private Secretary.

And that was it, apart from a few pleasantries. Politics, eh?

Within a few minutes the ticker tape at the bottom of the screen on the BBC News channel was reporting my appointment. Wow. It was real, after all.

How to break the news to Carolyn? I wanted her to be the first person I told. I picked up the Sky+ remote and froze the TV picture at the point where the ticker tape was announcing my appointment. Then a text message arrived: 'Congratulations, but you've made a lot of enemies.'

Suddenly, my elation was tempered. I looked at the message for a few seconds. So was this how it was going to be from now on? I had always valued my friendships at Westminster, always got on well with pretty much everyone. At least, I thought I did. Were things changing this much?

At first I wasn't going to respond at all. Then I thought better of it and typed: 'Your good wishes have touched my heart.'

I was impatient for Carolyn to return, but when she did I managed to pretend nothing unusual had happened. I helped her in with her shopping bags then nonchalantly told her there was something on the telly she might find interesting. She walked into the living room and stared for a few seconds at the frozen image on the TV screen, obviously confused as to what she should be seeing.

Then she gasped and turned to me, beaming. We actually started jumping up and down, laughing, and Ronnie joined in, though he had no idea what was going on. The noise made Reggie cry.

How do you solve a problem like Gordon?

By the time I'm lying on my death bed, many previously unanswerable questions may well have been answered: is there life elsewhere in the universe? Can global warming be reversed? John Barrowman – really?

But the question which I know will remain unanswered, even as I draw my final breath – preferably on the government benches of the House of Lords, but probably not – is: why did the Labour Party choose to lose the general election of 2010?

For choice it was; we chose to stick with Gordon Brown as our leader and Prime Minister, all the while knowing that we stood no chance of winning with him at the helm. Even today, after our inevitable humiliation, such a statement will be seen by some as disloyalty, which goes to show just how damaged and distorted debate became in the Labour Party during Gordon's leadership; to read the polls, to listen to what the voters were saying, to acknowledge that our choice of leader was less popular than the Tories' by a country mile – this sort of thing was disloyal. Apparently. Loyalty became defined as ignoring the bleeding obvious.

I hereby publicly admit my own culpability. I could have chosen, like a brave few other Labour MPs did, to follow my instincts and to refuse to nominate Gordon when Tony finally announced a date for his departure. But I had been a minister for only a few months and loved it. Did I really want to jeopardise my career by taking such a stand, when clearly GB was going to be elected leader unopposed anyway?

The answer, I now accept, is yes. But I was a coward. And I was not alone.

In my defence, I made it clear to at least one potential candidate – David Miliband – that I would nominate him if he chose to stand, and to hell with the consequences if GB took umbrage. Alas, David chose not to stand. As did Alan Milburn, Alan Johnson, John Reid and a few others who might have mounted a realistic, though probably unsuccessful, challenge.

Carolyn and I were in a Paris hotel on the Friday of Gordon's first reshuffle as Prime Minister. We were there to attend a Genesis concert the following evening – a Christmas gift from Carolyn who, with unerring good judgement, had decided that if she had to watch

Britain's greatest band with me (my opinion, not hers) she might as well get some shopping into the trip too. The new Prime Minister called me on my mobile at about seven in the evening.

GB: *Tom, you've been doing a great job at transport. I'd like you to continue in the job.*

Me: *Thank you, Prime Minister.*

GB: *(After a pause, then laughing) Don't call me that – call me Gordon!*

Me: *Yes, Gordon. Thank you.*

In fact, the call wasn't much of a surprise. I had already made it known to Gordon's people that, having served only ten months as railways minister, I wanted to continue for a while; the industry constantly suffers from a lack of continuity when it comes to political leadership.

And so began the Golden Weeks of Gordon's premiership, during which he appeared sure-footed and confident. One Sunday evening during that summer's floods crisis, I happened to be in London with Carolyn and the boys, so was asked to attend a meeting in Cabinet Office Briefing Room A (or Cobra, as the media love to call it, making it sound like an organisation James Bond might have had to deal with) to stand in for Ruth Kelly, the Transport Secretary. Being a fan of The West Wing, I was vaguely disappointed that all of us around the table didn't stand up when the Prime Minister breezed into the room. Nevertheless, Gordon was magnificent. He knew exactly what he wanted to ask and of whom (although I'm sure he glanced once in my direction and either didn't know who the hell I was or didn't know what I was doing there; I kept schtum). He chaired the meeting with a scary efficiency, leaving only after making sure everyone knew exactly what their orders were.

Having seen this decisive, bold leadership at close quarters, I felt some of my previous anxiety about Gordon's fitness for office recede.

And then, in October 2007, came The Election That Never Was – the defining moment from which Gordon's leadership never recovered. We would not take the lead in the polls again until it was far, far too late — after the disastrous 2010 general election.

By the summer of 2008, I was increasingly depressed by the prospect of Gordon leading us into the next election. Our poll deficit was alarming. We lost the Glasgow East by-election to the SNP, our first such defeat for twenty years. There were rumblings. Rumours were beginning to circulate that we might finally get the leadership contest we'd denied ourselves a year earlier. David Miliband wrote an incendiary piece for The Guardian, interpreted — accurately — as a throwing down of the gauntlet by the Foreign Secretary. I was in regular touch with the Scotland Office minister, the late David Cairns, one of my closest friends politically and personally, who was becoming increasingly unhappy; he wanted rid of Gordon just as much as I, but he was far more pessimistic that David Miliband or anyone else would have the guts to do anything about it. I was not as pessimistic. I was wrong. David was right.

An off-the-record briefing by David was reported by the BBC News Channel in terms that made it difficult for him subsequently to deny he was the source: a Minister of State was threatening to resign over Gordon's leadership. Fingers pointed at David, who was told by his Secretary of State, Des Browne, that all he had to do to stay in the job was to make a statement saying he had full confidence in Gordon's leadership.

David resigned.

And this is where my blog undoubtedly quickened the demise of my own career, to a far greater extent than the silly faux outrage that greeted my 'Heaven knows we're miserable now' post a few months earlier.

When I heard the news that David had resigned, he was in Glasgow doing a single, pooled interview for the broadcast outlets. I phoned him to invite him and his partner, Dermot, to ours for dinner. I was concerned that if he went home to Greenock he might have media doorstepping him all night. And also, I wanted a gossip.

'You don't mind me being seen in public arriving at your house?' asked David.

'Is Dermot with you?'

'Yes.'

'Well, get him to throw a jumper over your face before you arrive.'

Maybe I was feeling a bit ashamed that my friend had taken a principled stand and I hadn't. Certainly I was fully aware that David might well come in for the McBride Treatment, that Number 10 might start briefing God knows what about him. Time for some solidarity, I thought. And so, before he arrived, I quickly wrote and published the following post.

David Cairns

Published: September 16, 2008

David Cairns was one of my closest friends, inside or outside politics. His tragic and premature death from acute pancreatitis in May 2011 was a devastating blow to everyone who knew and loved him.

David Cairns is one of my closest friends in politics. He was also one of the most effective ministers I have ever known — astute judgement, common sense by the bucketful, impressive political instinct and extremely sharp and witty at the despatch box. He is also fiercely loyal; he's never voted against the government or criticised it publicly.

I know that he loved being a minister, that he regarded it as an immense privilege, which of course it is.

And I know that until this morning he had no intention of resigning. But being named by *The Daily Telegraph* as the Minister of State who was the subject of News 24's report last night forced his hand.

When he says he is not part of a wider conspiracy to topple the Prime Minister, he is telling the truth.

David's decision was one he reached with a huge amount of regret and he will be devastated. But it was also a decision based on honesty and principle and he deserves respect for what he has done, even from those of us who would have preferred him not to follow this particular course of action.

Named and (not particularly) shamed

Published: September 21, 2008

Journalists are really scraping the bottom of the barrel to try to get new angles on the 'leadership crisis' story. Today's *Sunday Times* names me as risking 'censure' by expressing sympathy with David Cairns.

Well, if 'Minister still friends with former minister' qualifies as a story, then British journalism really is going down the pan.

David had never once suggested to me that I should resign; I still don't believe he would have chosen that particular moment to go either. But there were others who were blatantly calling ministers urging them to resign and to create a leadership crisis. Siobhan McDonagh, the Mitcham and Morden MP, and a close friend (and former employer) of David's had resigned earlier in the summer as a whip with that very intention, as had a number of party 'vice chairs', such as Joan Ryan and Barry Gardiner. But David's was the first ministerial resignation.

My view was clear and, I think, in retrospect, sound: I would happily resign in order to support a rival candidate to Gordon; what I would not do is resign in the forlorn hope that someone in the Cabinet might at some point grow a pair, leaving me on the backbenches and Gordon still at Number 10. No, if a challenger emerged, I would support him. If not, tough.

By September 2008 the pressures of the ministerial job, combined with my constituency duties, was taking its toll on the family. Carolyn was amazing, getting on with managing the boys and the house, while trying to hold down her own job, all while being, for most of the week, a single parent. With David's resignation, the prospect of a move to the non-job of Minister of State at the Scotland Office was raised. While being far less satisfying than the DfT, the job would have given me more time in Scotland and, I hoped, at home.

So when David and Dermot arrived at the house on that September evening for Chinese food, champagne (Dermot was celebrating getting a new job) and moral support, I warned David that if GB called to offer me his job (David's, not Gordon's, obviously), I would take it. Since neither he nor I had intended to resign at this precise moment anyway. He understood. But the call never came and instead Ann McKechin, my colleague representing Glasgow North, filled that vacancy, now relegated back to Parliamentary Under-Secretary of State grade.

Conference two weeks later was hectic. Aside from the febrile rumour-mongering, hints of plots, ostentatious and enthusiastic declarations of loyalty, it was the busiest conference I had had since attending as a staffer in 1992. Very few railways ministers had stayed in post long enough to attend three consecutive party conferences in the role, but in 2008 I had achieved just that.

In hindsight, it's now difficult to understand why I was surprised by my sacking a week later. In the bar in one of the conference hotels, I was buttonholed by a high-profile Brownite and asked about my blogpost in support of David.

'Not your finest moment, Tom. Why did you do it?'

'To fire a shot across Number 10's bows.'

'Meaning what?'

'To warn them off from briefing against David.'

'Who would do that?'

'Damien McBride.'

'That's crap! Damien's never briefed against anyone!'

Hmm.

And as he walked out of the bar, he pointed at me and said: 'Bad move, mate.'

And so it turned out to be.

The call

Published: October 3, 2008

Okay, I admit that was a bit of a shock to the system. GB called five minutes ago and the bottom line is ... hello again, back bench!

More later, once I've had a chance to ruminate.

UPDATE at 9.40pm: Carolyn reckons she's worked out the reasoning behind my sacking. She's just drawn my attention to a strapline on BBC News that says: 'Brown: We need serious people for serious times.'

D'oh!

Kind words that mean a lot
Published: October 4, 2008

Some people have been leaving very nice and supportive messages since I got The Call. Some not so nice, but there you are.

If what follows were to be my political epitaph, however, I could hardly expect anything better. It was posted as a comment last night under the name 'Very Much Anonymous', and you'll see the reason for that in the last line. I hope one day this particular individual will make him/herself known to me. But in the meantime, whoever you are, thank you.

Tom, I'm very sorry to hear this news.

I'm not a Labour supporter and I won't be voting Labour at the next election. However, I know that most politicians of any political persuasion genuinely want to do their best to help their constituents and the people of the UK. You exemplify this.

You have, from all the evidence available to me, been a conscientious and hard-working Minister. You've handled a difficult portfolio extremely well and have built up a lot of respect on a personal level within the rail industry. I am sure that the industry's journals will decry your treatment for weeks to come.

You have been courteous to and respectful of your officials. You ask intelligent questions at the right time and you have a remarkable talent to sense when you are being 'fed a line', be it by officials or by industry figures.

Your blog has opened up the political process to the average citizen more than any other. While Iain Dale and Guido write superb blogs, they don't have the perspective that you do.

It is my sincere belief that your party will lose the next election by a large margin. However, despite my Conservative sympathies, I distrust large majorities. I sincerely hope that you will continue with both your blog and your devotion to your job and will hold governments of both parties to account from the back benches.

More than that, after the next election, your party will need a core group of experienced but untainted leaders to pull it out of a very deep hole. You have the potential to go far higher within your party than you have managed to date. Please don't let this setback discourage you.

Why do I say this?

Because I've been working for you in DfT for quite some time. Hence why I'm staying anonymous.

From ministerial Mondeo to back bench
Published: October 12, 2008

The *Mail on Sunday* have today published a slightly edited version of an article they commissioned from me on the subject of how a minister is sacked and adjusts to his new life, a subject I feel eminently qualified to discuss.

You can't read MoS's online version (in the *Review* section) without paying to register on its site, apparently, but below is my original draft; the 'director's cut', if you will:

> The classic Motown song, 'This Old Heart of Mine' by the Isley Brothers, is the default ringtone on my phone, and at precisely 7.50pm it started to play as 'number withheld' appeared on the display. Having just put my two young sons to bed, I was getting changed out of my suit in the spare bedroom. Still in a state of partial undress, I answered the call.
>
> 'This is the Number 10 switchboard. Can you hold for the Prime Minister?'
>
> Well, there aren't too many answers to that question, are there? I walked downstairs clutching the phone to my ear and went into the kitchen where my wife, Carolyn, was making a late dinner. 'Number 10,' I mouthed silently at her, and she immediately switched off the blaring radio.
>
> The received wisdom about reshuffles is that if you're going to get sacked, it's done early on in the day. Having heard nothing so far, I was pretty confident that a call this late in the day would surely mean promotion. I knew I had done a good job at transport. I also knew that Minister of State in that department was now vacant. Or immigration, perhaps? Europe even?
>
> And with such optimistic expectancy did I take the call from the Prime Minister. The conversation was brief: he was bringing new people into the government, and that meant some people would have to leave. My heart sank,

my stomach lurched and I made a 'thumbs-down' gesture to Carolyn, who mouthed a word that ladies shouldn't really utter.

Later on, I would think of clever retorts and witty one-liners, such as 'Oh, bloody hell, Gordon!' But at the time I was so shell-shocked, I merely acquiesced in his request that I 'step aside' for the greater good of the government. I'm not entirely sure but I may even have said 'Thanks for calling...'

That same morning a courier had delivered a ministerial red box, heavy with unsigned letters and policy submissions for my approval. Suddenly, in the space of a single telephone conversation, I had been transformed from a minister of the crown to a backbench MP with no authority even to open the box, let alone read any of its contents.

Carolyn's sense of irony never deserts her, and that evening she insisted we crack open a bottle of champagne.

Until then, I had been in government, in one role or another, for five years. Before becoming a minister, I had been Parliamentary Private Secretary (PPS) to Northern Ireland minister John Spellar (2003–2005), then PPS to Health Secretary Patricia Hewitt (2005–2006). In September 2006, I turned down an invitation from fellow backbenchers to sign a letter requesting that Tony Blair resign as Prime Minister. A minister who did add his name was forced to resign as a result, and the ensuing mini-reshuffle brought me into the government as a minister at the Department for Transport (DfT).

To this day I have never regretted refusing to sign that letter; and being appointed as a minister by Tony Blair remains the proudest moment of my political life.

As a minister, at least while Parliament was sitting, I would leave my Glasgow home at 6.30am on a Monday in order to catch the 7.10am train to Euston. The first silver lining of my sacking became apparent on the following Monday when I caught the 3.10pm train after spending a relaxed morning and afternoon with Carolyn and the boys.

There had been no vote in the Commons that evening, but I wanted to pop in on the Strangers' bar anyway to see friends and colleagues, some of whom I hadn't seen since the start of the recess. The sympathy at what had happened was encouraging and touching, as was the invariable expression of indignation at the unfairness of it. I was determined to be philosophical: these things have happened before and they will happen again.

But when it came to going home time, I received another shock to the system: I had no ministerial car to drop me at my flat. It had been two years since I had had to make my own way home; would I know the way by myself? Should I phone my old driver, Bob, and ask him for directions?

But the Harrises are nothing if not resourceful and I managed to get safely home. The next morning, emerging from the flat after an unaccustomed long lie-in, I instinctively looked round for the familiar brown Mondeo. My heart sank when I realised it was never going to be there again.

It's not a particularly long walk into the Commons from where I live in Pimlico, and I found myself enjoying the 'fresh' air of central London as I contemplated the day ahead. A normal day at the Department for Transport would have started with breakfast at the Commons followed by back-to-back meetings at Great Minster

House, the odd set-piece speech somewhere in London or even a ministerial visit outside London. From first meeting to last vote would regularly be about thirteen or fourteen hours. Today I didn't even have to look at my diary to see what lay ahead of me now: breakfast, office time, meeting with my researcher, office time, lunch with blogger Iain Dale, coffee with a journalist, office time...

Sometime soon I will get back into a backbench routine, but in the immediate aftermath of being sacked, it's hard to adjust to a regime where your time isn't ruthlessly carved up by a small army of efficient civil servants.

I will miss that 'small army' immensely. I had four full-time members of my ministerial private office. I could also rely on a much bigger army of DfT officials whose advice and knowledge was impressive and daunting.

My former private secretary, Rachel, phoned me to discuss tying up 'loose ends'. I didn't fancy going back into the department, at least not yet. So she met me in Central Lobby of the Houses of Parliament and I reluctantly handed over the keys to my red box and my departmental security pass. I returned to my office in the upper committee corridor divested of the final vestiges of ministerial authority.

The most common theory put forward for my sacking is, inevitably, my blog, *And Another Thing...* In some ways, this is comforting: no one really believes I was bad at my job so there must be another reason, and the blog is a prime suspect, especially after the whole 'Why is everyone so bloody miserable?' debacle.

I started it in March this year because I was concerned that right-wing blogs like Iain Dale's and Guido Fawkes's were dominating the market, and I felt there weren't enough Labour voices out there.

Few people were even aware I wrote a blog until 'Why is everyone so bloody miserable' was published in June. What started off as a fairly thoughtful piece about the difficulty of achieving happiness in a material world was twisted by a Conservative frontbencher to try to make it look like I was belittling people's real difficulties in coping with the current economic climate. I found myself having to defend and explain what I had written to hostile journalists and broadcasters. It was a sharp reminder that, even if the public aren't reading a minister's blog, journalists and political opponents are.

Even then, I received no criticism from Number 10; my boss at the time, Ruth Kelly, simply asked how I was coping with the media scrum.

And you can go over my posts with a fine tooth comb and you won't find anything there that's off-message or critical of government policy.

But I hope the blog wasn't the reason for my sacking. I wouldn't like to think that any minister who makes a serious attempt to have a dialogue with voters, who tries to communicate Labour's agenda to the public and who (God help us) makes jokes at his own expense is immediately regarded as a loose canon. Surely voters prefer their politicians to sound as if they're at least familiar with the planet Earth? And what's more off-putting than a minister who sounds as if he's reciting a Labour Party press release he's memorised an hour earlier?

I'm not naive; I know that there are some senior politicians who don't think it's necessarily appropriate for a minister to write about what his favourite karaoke performances are ('Home' by Michael Bublé and 'Turning Japanese' by the Vapors), or who thinks he will win *The X-Factor* (Austin), or to write a review of the entire fourth season of *Doctor Who* (best yet – better to come).

And I'm sure not everyone in the Labour Party thinks I should publish comments from readers of my blog which are critical of me, the government or the party.

But I genuinely believe that blogs can and will be an important part of the political debate in this country in the future. And I happen to think that ministers, as well as ordinary party members, should be saying something interesting and challenging and – yes – human to the increasing numbers who are logging on to read them.

I like to think *And Another Thing...* would have continued even if I had remained in government; it will certainly continue now that I'm not. Whether people will want to read it now that it's written by a backbencher, and not a minister, is another matter.

But if it wasn't the blog, and it wasn't incompetence, then what? Politics?

The fact is, I don't know. No one is ever told.

And sometimes, when the music stops, there just isn't a chair for you. It can be as simple as that and you just have to accept it.

The stalking horse scenario

A few weeks before the European elections of June 2009, I found myself on a train heading home. With me were a handful of parliamentary colleagues who I knew but not very well. They represented seats mainly, though not entirely, in the north of England. Discussion turned to Gordon, and it quickly became apparent that not a single one of us wanted him to remain as leader, though no one was optimistic that he would step down voluntarily before the election.

This was of some interest to me because, although I knew well the various shades of GB-related opinion among my closest colleagues, this was the first time the subject had been broached by others outside my own circle. For the first time I felt vaguely hopeful that GB might yet be deposed.

At about this time I spoke to two Tory friends, one an MP. When I suggested we might go into the election – albeit an early one – with Alan Johnson as our leader rather than GB, their faces physically fell. The sure and certain prospect that their man Cameron would fail to beat a Johnson-led Labour Party filled them with horror. I hope you're wrong, they both told me with sincerity.

A few days after my informative train journey, I had a cup of tea with Barry Gardiner, the MP for Brent North, who had resigned as Gordon's 'tree envoy' or something similarly meaningless a year earlier and was now Parliamentary Private Secretary (PPS) to Lord Mandelson. I told Barry of my conversation with our colleagues aboard the train and, in a conspiratorial manner, he suggested he set up a meeting in which I could discuss my concerns with the President of the Board of Trade.

Now, I had had, up to that point, approximately two conversations with Peter Mandelson in my entire life. The first was when, as outgoing

Director of Communications for the Labour Party in September 1990, he had welcomed me aboard as the Scottish party's first ever full-time press officer. The second had been at conference shortly after being selected as a parliamentary candidate and just before the 2001 election, and even then I only stopped to speak to him because Carolyn was with me and she wanted to meet him.

So why did Barry now think it would be fruitful to relate my reservations about Gordon to someone who had been brought back into the government with the sole intention of propping up his leadership?

I was surprised to find that I was one of about four Labour MPs who met with Peter in his Lords office a few days later. I was even more surprised to find that the subject under discussion was not the leadership crisis (and Gordon's leadership was in crisis permanently between October 2007 and May 2010) but the government's planned part-privatisation of Royal Mail. Supported by his talented deputy, Pat McFadden, Peter eloquently and convincingly put the case for the legislation, easily dealing with the concerns expressed by the others present. Clearly this was a meeting aimed at reassuring those mostly loyal MPs who had expressed reservations about the plans.

I enjoyed the discussion and took some small part in it, but began to wonder why I had been invited in the first place. Then, as everyone filed out, Barry said to Peter: 'Tom would like a quick word with you before you leave.'

Although I hadn't been prepared to make a 'pitch', there was nothing else for it but to be very direct. 'Peter, the majority of the PLP has lost confidence in Gordon. He has to go.'

Peter looked at me for a few seconds, as a fox might consider a very tall and nervous chicken. He didn't say anything immediately, so I filled the gap. 'I know you're loyal to Gordon—'

And at that he interrupted with: 'I would never say anything critical of Gordon publicly.'

Even at the time I thought that an interesting choice of words.

He thanked me for approaching him and I left. And that was that. Until...

Campaigning in the European Parliament elections of 2009 was probably one of the worst political experiences of my life. As the MPs' expenses scandal erupted from every front page, I had to knock on doors to ask voters to come out and vote Labour. The reception was less than welcoming, even in my own Labour heartlands. All politicians were seen as venal, grasping crooks, but it was Labour who were in government and it was Labour who were taking most of the blame.

On polling day, I spoke by phone to Jane Kennedy, the Liverpool Wavertree MP and an all round good egg who I had tried unsuccessfully to persuade to stand for deputy leader two years earlier. Jane told me that one of the (many) rumours doing the rounds that day was that a member of the Cabinet was preparing to announce his or her resignation as polls closed that night. Who could it be? The chances were no one. But if it was true, it could have been anyone. Apart from the few Brownites in the Praetorian Guard, disenchantment with GB was widespread, even within the Cabinet.

When news broke at precisely ten o'clock that James Purnell, the Work and Pensions Secretary, was leaving the Cabinet, I punched the air in triumph. Surely this was the end? All it would take was one more big beast to announce his or her resignation and we would finally be back in the game, finally be in with a chance of depriving the Tories of the electoral prize they assumed to be their birthright.

A rumour that David Miliband was considering his position was reported on Sky. Surely this was too good to be true?

Yes. Yes, it was.

Two colleagues for whom I have a huge amount of respect – Jim Knight, the then education minister, and Caroline Flint, the then housing minister – appeared in front of the cameras to offer their undying support for Gordon. Then, as I was losing the will to live, it was reported that David Miliband would not, after all, be resigning and was pledging his full support to Gordon. Again.

Was it all over? I went to bed feeling angry and depressed. The next day was dominated by news of James's resignation and the rather belated and confused resignation of Caroline Flint. Then Jane

Kennedy announced she was also leaving in protest at Gordon's leadership style. Gordon held a press conference at which he insisted he never had any intention of replacing Alistair Darling with Ed Balls. There is no record of anyone believing this.

I was becoming increasingly angry. I was taking it personally. Carolyn had rarely seen me so down. Why was this happening? My party, the party of government, had secured barely 17 per cent of the vote in a national election! It would have been bad enough if others didn't share my analysis, if they genuinely believed that Gordon was the best person to lead us into the election. But surely no one actually believed that, whatever they might say on the record in order to hold onto their ministerial cars?

I'm not one of life's resigners, but it is something of a comfort to know that my sacking in October 2008 only cut short my ministerial career by eight months, because it would have been utterly impossible to remain in post − even if I'd been given the choice − after James had shown the courage and leadership I was desperate for others to show.

So it was with a particularly heavy heart that I went to Glasgow Central on the Monday morning to head back to London. Carolyn had given me a lift and we went for a coffee to pass the time until my train was ready.

The thing about Carolyn − and I'm sure she won't mind my saying this − is that she isn't one for conviction politics. Had I stayed in post long enough to resign on principle, she would not have approved. Let someone else put their head above the parapet, would have been her advice.

But she knew how unhappy I had been over that awful weekend and she understood that I had to make a stand in some form or other.

We had often joked about the Stalking Horse Scenario. That's what we insignificant backbenchers call ourselves when we consider having a go at the top job: a stalking horse. We call ourselves that because we know we won't be taken seriously and we need to let everyone else know that we don't expect to be taken seriously. Otherwise everyone will say, 'What, you? Seriously?'

That morning in Glasgow Central, despite maintaining a consistent policy of advising me not to put my head above the parapet, Carolyn actually said: 'I wouldn't be so strongly against you standing as a stalking horse now.'

This was a true sign of love. She absolutely hated the idea of putting herself and the boys in the media firing line; there's only so many times you can tolerate opening the front door to a journalist and photographer from the Mail on Sunday. *And she knew there was a high risk of being utterly humiliated – not in an actual leadership contest, but in not even getting enough MP nominations to get a contest going.*

Even as she said it, though, it wasn't a serious prospect. The moment of danger for GB had already passed. If the resignation of a prominent Cabinet minister wasn't going to budge Gordon, then the futile windmill-tilting activities of an obscure backbencher was hardly going to bring him crashing down.

But that night, Gordon would be addressing the Parliamentary Labour Party. I would have my say then.

During the journey south, I rehearsed over and over what I was going to say. It had to be short and to the point. I would displease many of my colleagues, but I no longer cared. The party I loved and to which I had devoted most of my adult life was about to suffer an utterly needless electoral disaster and I was not going to go along with that project out of misplaced loyalty.

The train broke down and, along with two colleagues with whom I'd been traveling, I jumped in a taxi to the next station to recommence the journey southwards. In the taxi, my mobile rang.

'Is that Tom Harris?'

'Speaking.'

'This is the switchboard at Number 10. Please hold for Peter Mandelson.'

I suddenly remembered that the reshuffle was still underway. A short silence, then Peter's voice: 'Tom, I was recalling our conversation a few weeks ago and afterwards, I spoke to some people and asked them why this talented young man wasn't a minister.'

'Well, I used to be.'

'Why were you sacked?'

'I have no idea. You should ask Gordon.'

'And if I were to arrange it so that you were brought back in to the government now?'

I was speechless. Why was this happening? I loved being a minister and desperately wanted to return to office. But in the current circumstances?

'Sorry, Peter. I can't accept.'

'Why not?' He sounded surprised and annoyed.

'Because I would be betraying my friends.'

'Who?'

'James Purnell and Jane Kennedy, for a start.'

'Oh, okay.'

And that was that.

I felt close to tears, to be honest. I sat in the cab as it trundled to our destination, feeling genuinely shell-shocked. Had the offer been genuine? What was the job anyway? Peter hadn't mentioned a specific post. And why Peter? Since when did the Secretary of State for Trade and Industry have the authority to hand out jobs in the Prime Minister's stead?

I made the mistake of phoning Carolyn to tell her what had happened. A few minutes later she texted me to tell me she was 'proud and angry' in equal measure. A few days later the balance had shifted in favour of 'angry'.

By the time our delayed train arrived at Euston, I barely had any time before the start of the PLP. But I got a good seat, on the back row opposite the entrance, about half way down the room from where Gordon would speak. Worryingly, Don Touhig, MP for Islwyn, and a Brownite loyalist, sat next to me. Even more worryingly, Tommy McAvoy, the feared and respected pairing whip and another devout Brownite, sat on the other side of him.

Gordon arrived to the inevitable cheering and applause, which is always organised for any failing or failed leader for the benefit of the hacks outside the room who have their ears pressed against the door.

Perhaps I'm being unfair. Perhaps the enthusiasm was a reflection of our tremendous achievement in hitting double figures in the share of the vote a day earlier. Who knows?

I raised my hand to catch the chair, Tony Lloyd's, eye. He nodded. There was no going back now. Tony read out the names of those he intended to call. I was second or third.

Prime Minister's question
Published: June, 8 2009

I don't intend to allow this blog to become an anti-Gordon Brown platform, so I'll say what I have to say in the hope of not having to return to the subject.

I made a contribution to tonight's PLP, along these lines:

> If there's one thing that unites this PLP it's a determination to win the next election. And those of us who have come to the conclusion, by an entirely objective and logical process, that you cannot lead Labour to victory, would be doing a disservice to our country and to our party by staying silent. The results from last night have confirmed in my mind that the electorate aren't yet sold on Cameron, but they have made their minds up about you, Gordon, and it's not going to change. We can win the next election, but only if we have a new leader. So answer me this, Gordon: Why do you think Cameron wants you to remain in post?

I have no intention of becoming a media tart on this issue (on any other issue that would be fine, obviously). I've done some media this evening but after today, that's it.

I'll give you one reason why I love the PLP. In the eyes of many present, I had just committed an act of treason. I could expect to suffer a degree of animosity for a time, perhaps forever, from certain individuals. But apart from John Prescott shouting contemptuously, 'Stick to the blogging!' the only hostility I perceived in the immediate aftermath of my contribution was Don, sitting beside me, saying loudly, 'Dear, oh dear!'

I then made a mistake: I agreed to do media interviews, including an interview, along with fellow Brown-sceptic Barry Sheerman, by Paxo on Newsnight. Although the wider public had a legitimate interest in the future of Brown as Prime Minister, it was his position as leader of my party I had challenged. Taking that dispute outside of Committee Room 14 was seen by some in the party to cross the line from internal democratic debate to publicly undermining the government, and I came quickly to regret doing that – the media interviews, that is, not the calling on Brown to go...

Whimsy

Hangin' with the kids
Published: June 26, 2008

To the north east this morning to unveil a plaque and make a speech to mark the opening of a new roads project. Numerous children were in attendance and presented a pleasant antidote to all the middle-aged men in suits (me, for instance).

But what do you say to a ten-year-old who's been press ganged into sharing a photo opportunity with the minister?

'So, did you see *Doctor Who* last week?'

'What?'

'*Doctor Who*. Did you see it last week? You know, with the beetle and the nuclear explosion and stuff.'

Blank expression. Embarrassed silence.

Photographer shouts: 'Smile, please!'

Another embarrassed silence. I am the minister, after all. I should engage with young people.

'Davros is in it this week.'

'Who?'

'Creator of the Daleks.'

'Oh, right. Cool.'

More silence.

'Thank you,' yells the photographer.

My young interlocutor strolls back to his mates without so much as a backwards glance, undoubtedly impressed with how down with the kids and in touch with youth culture that surprisingly youthful minister is.

Booyakasha. As it were.

Haltemprice & Howden: an armchair guide
Published: June 25, 2008

To the bewilderment of parliament, the media and the country, former Tory leadership contender David Davis resigned as shadow Foreign

Secretary in order to fight a by-election on the issue of Labour's civil liberties record, particularly its policy of detaining terrorist suspects without charge for up to 42-days.

Turnout in Haltemprice and Howden at the 2005 election was just a smidgeon over 70 per cent. If turnout at the forthcoming by-election is a single vote less than that, David Davis's kamikaze moment will all have been for nothing.

Here's a turnout scorecard to help you gauge his success:

70–80 per cent: Well done, David. You're a popular guy in your constituency but most people in the country still support 42-days

60–70 per cent: Oh, dear. Still, never mind, you're back in a job at least.

50–60 per cent: Er, remind me why you did this?

40–50 per cent: You do know you're not getting back on the front bench, don't you?

30–40 per cent: 'Here he comes – quick, look the other way!'

An old joke, but a good one
Published: July 7, 2008

A Labour activist is walking along a cliff-top path, when he sees two people clinging by their fingertips to the edge. Turns out that one is a Tory and the other is a Liberal Democrat. So the moral dilemma is this: which one does the Labour Party member kick off first? The answer? The Tory – business before pleasure…

You can use that one if you want.

Not funny. Seriously.

Published: July 20, 2008

I disapprove, of course, but I couldn't help finding this headline over at 'The Daily Mash' very funny:

'GOVERNMENT TO CONSOLIDATE ALL ITS DEBTS INTO ONE LOW MONTHLY PAYMENT'

LOL (but only if that means 'Laugh out loud'; if it actually means 'Lots of love' then ignore it because it's not appropriate).

'David' feels our pain – live as it happens

Published: October 1, 2008

I've decided to try my hand at writing an open thread, *à la* Iain Dale, on the Great Leader's speech as it happens. Any comments, as always, gratefully received...

2.35: Louise Bagshawe's doing the introduction. Isn't she a fiction writer? Oh, right, I get it. And she's getting a lot of applause by suggesting a return to Thatcherism. Oh, and she's not introducing 'David', but another PPC. Only about 620 more to go before he comes on, then...

2.41: We're at the candidate for Clwyd South now. 'Thanks for coming to see me.' Good gag.

2.44: Oh, excellent! Davina Rankin's on – she's up against me next time!

2.46: Another one? Oh, come on! I was told 2.30...

2.49: William 'interesting' Roache is in the audience. Why didn't he say something?

2.49: The *whole* shadow Cabinet? Are they all going to speak?

2.51: What, are they just playing for time now? Is DC stuck on a bus somewhere or something?

2.54: I feel a bit out of touch. Is the whole shadow Cabinet doing community service or something?

2.55: It's Dr Fox. Still hasn't got over being dropped from *The X-Factor*, I see. Nice tribute to our armed forces, though. Good line about role models.

2.56: Another video. We need more of this kind of thing – pride in our armed forces, rather than banning them from recruiting in schools.

3.00: At last, here he is. Was that a bus pass I saw him slipping back into his pocket? Nice tie – good start.

3.01: Straight into the financial situation with a call for bipartisanship. He's taking credit for the plan to raise savings guarantee to £50,000. That little piece of bipartisanship must have lasted nearly eight seconds.

3.03: 'Decisions in past ten years led us to this point.' So, back to partisan politics, then? Fair enough.

3.05: Good line on Afghanistan.

3.06: He's using notes. Good. Always thought that was a distracting gimmick.

3.07: Returning soldiers being refused services? That happened once and he received an apology. Come off it, Dave. Poor.

3.09: Conservative values. 'Many people think Conservative values are just about freedom.' Er, no we don't Dave. At least he's distancing himself from the libertarian weirdos.

3.12: A bit of a pause there when he expected applause and it didn't come quickly enough. Oh, here comes his 'novice' defence...

3.13: Defending the Union – loud applause. Okay, I'm glad about that. I'm guessing there's a 'but' coming up, though...

3.14: Apple pie and motherhood. Controversial and brave (sarcasm).

3.15: 'We will need to do difficult and unpopular things.' Well, you're a Tory, what else would you do?

3.16: The character and judgement line. 'Broken society.' 'Change.' And there's Maggie getting another namecheck and the loudest applause so far. Interesting...

3.18: Reasonably decent 'balcony' joke at GB's expense (he wrote grudgingly).

3.20: Attack on city slickers. GB responsible for world financial crisis, apparently.

3.21: Ah, here we go with the attacks on public spending. We were wrong to spend on health and education. Wonder if he'll say how much less we should have spent?

3.22: No.

3.23: William 'interesting' Roache looks bored.

3.26: Just had to answer the door for my Tesco delivery. Did I miss anything?

3.28: 'Labour's taxes are making it impossible for entrepreneurs.' OK, so a tax cut promise coming up, then? Well…?

3.29: Corporation tax to be cut by 3pc. Does GO know about this? Didn't he say no tax cuts?

3.30: No to Heathrow's third runway? There's no way he actually believes that.

3.32: Seems to be claiming Labour doesn't believe in society! There's no way he actually believes that.

3.33: Attacking the 'human rights' culture. And the bit about an officer not being allowed to pursue an armed criminal is just made up, Dave.

3.35: Attacking MPs' expenses. This is pure dog whistle politics.

3.38: Where hospitals are closing it's to take advantage of economies of scale, to improve service delivery. Under the Tories, when hospitals closed, it was because they didn't have enough money. Get real, Dave.

3.40: Attacking the government's record on MRSA. Unfortunately, we weren't able, in Opposition, to attack his government's record on MRSA. Mainly because they refused to keep records on it. Wonder why?

3.43: 'We are now the party of the NHS.' We just won't say how much less we would have spent on it had we been in government.

3.43: The broken society again. No mention yet of the deliberate creation of the underclass by the Tories in order to keep unemployment figures down. I'm sure it's coming up.

3.47: State intervention grudgingly accepted.

3.48: He's just promised to scrap something but I'm not sure what.

3.49: Supports flexible working. Good.

3.50: Here we go – if you're thinking of divorcing because you can no longer stand the sight of your partner, don't do anything hasty because Dave's going to give you a tenner a month to stay together. Crack open that bubbly!

3.52: I'm getting hungry. Wonder if there are any snacks in that Tesco delivery?

3.53: I agree with him on the 'all must have prizes' nonsense. Not sure what that means in terms of policy, though.

3.54: I didn't know there was a Spelling Society, never mind a president of it. But of course, Dave's right on this. And on the 'F*** off' thing.

3.56: Dave's lecturing us on the benefit culture his party initiated. Genius.

3.58: 'We've made the Conservative Party the party of social justice.' No you haven't, mate.

3.59: Carolyn's just discovered that while I've been blogging, Reggie scoffed nearly a whole box of Cadbury's chocolate fingers. I'm toast.

4.00: 'You didn't take international development seriously…' True.

4.01: If we don't accept the Tories have changed, then that means we haven't changed. Apparently. I honestly don't know what that means.

4.02: Wonder what's on the other channel?

4.03: The word 'peroration' is flashing at the bottom of the screen.

4.04: Thank goodness that's over. Not his best. Maybe he should have used an autocue?

Well, that was fun.

The modern dilemma
Published: October 14, 2008

OK, so here's the problem: I'm sitting in the Quiet Zone of a Virgin Pendolino and a bloke who got on at Carlisle has been talking very loudly into his phone. So, knowing that, since this is Britain, no one will say anything to him (opting instead for the well-worn and much-loved strategy of rolling one's eyes and tutting barely audibly) I decide to walk over and have a friendly chat.

Me: 'Excuse me, but you do know you're in the Quiet Zone?'
Bloke with phone: 'Yes, I read the sign.'
Me: 'Okay… But that doesn't really explain why you were on the phone, does it?'
Bloke with annoyed look on his face: 'Point taken.'
Me: 'Okay, then.'
So now I'm sitting here, nervously expecting him at any moment to make another call, just to send a signal that he won't be told what to do by annoying Scotspersons. And what do I do

then? Others in the carriage saw and heard me speak to him the first time; they'll expect me to say something, won't they?

I have a number of options if this happens:

1. Ignore him, thereby establishing beyond doubt that I am less than a man, worthy only of disdain. But then, I'm an MP, so I'm kind of used to that.
2. I could walk past his table, grab his phone, run through the train at full speed and try to flush it down the chemical toilet. This course of action could actually result in the first proper fight I've been in since 1975, not to mention the prospect of a large amount of media coverage round about the same time as my trial.
3. I could pretend I was only travelling as far as Preston and get out there.
4. I could shove a DVD into my laptop and plug in my earphones – then he could talk all he wants and I wouldn't know or care.

Any other suggestions gratefully received.

Sentences you don't expect to hear #66
Published: November 3, 2008

During a recent car journey with two of my constituency staff, a natural lull in the conversation developed before Malcolm, *á propos* of nothing, said: 'I was once chased round Turriff pool by some girls who thought I was the drummer out of the Bay City Rollers.'

The silence returned.

Sometimes it's better not to ask.

Smiling through the tears
Published: November 13, 2008

Following on from my earlier post about the Post Office, I was discussing the issue tonight with Craig, one of my oldest friends as well as the funniest person I know. He said he had recently used a Post Office branch to pre-approve his passport application. But when he showed his photo to the member of staff, he was told it probably wouldn't be accepted because he was smiling in it.

'No I'm not, it's a neutral expression.'

'No, you're smiling, I can see your teeth. You shouldn't be smiling.'

Pause.

'Does it help that I'm crying on the inside?'

In the event his photo was approved.

Words of wisdom
Published: November 18, 2008

Cabinet Office Minister, Liam Byrne, was mocked for writing a memo to his civil servants explaining what he wanted served with his morning cappuccino, along with various other 'helpful' hints on how to deal with him.

I think it's time I came clean. A Freedom of Information request has been received for the memo below, so I figured I would simply publish it now rather than allow it to come out at some later date. I wrote it on the day I was appointed as a minister and I reckon the advice to civil servants has stood the test of time.

MEMO: 6 September 2006
Understanding 'The joy of Tom'

1. First of all, congratulations on having me as a minister. I'm sure you deserve it.

2. How to address me: my friends call me 'Tom' or 'Darling'. You may call me 'Sir' or, occasionally (on more informal occasions) 'Minister'.

3. Deep fried Mars bars – I expect these to be provided in large quantities before, during and after every meeting. Chips optional.

4. Whenever I say 'optional' you should interpret that as 'mandatory'.

5. My hilarious red 'Jimmy' wig should be available for me to use at any speaking event. Good at breaking ice. (NOTE: Not for use in the Commons, not after that last time.)

6. Lunch – no fresh fruit or vegetables, please (unless you count potatoes which have been sliced and deep fried).

7. Red boxes – Occasionally I will want a red box at home over the weekend, but only so I can hold it up and pretend I'm the Chancellor of the Exchequer. So don't put anything in it, because they're already heavy enough.

8. When officials brief me on anything they must speak very, very slowly and not use big words. They must

interpret my blank, confused stares as follow-up questions.

9. I will express my enthusiasm for, and interest in, any subject with ostentatious yawning, stretching, looking at my watch and sleeping.

10. If I appear to faint at the despatch box, don't panic: this is simply a clever strategy I have devised for avoiding difficult questions in the Commons. It's not mentioned in 'Erskine May' so is therefore allowed under the rules of the House.

11. I am excellent very much good to express self in writing words so would liking to speech writing also me. But only sometimes.

12. If you need to contact me during the weekend for any purpose, don't bother. My mobile will be switched off and if you phone me on my home number I will answer in a fake foreign accent and pretend to sound confused and sullen.

13. Most importantly, get used to me being around for a long time to come. Thanks to the insightful wisdom expressed in my blog, I'm confident that, come the next reshuffle, I'll be promoted either within the department or to another department, in which case, the luckier members of staff can come with me.

Warning by H.M. Government:
Christmas can seriously damage your health

Published: December 23, 2008

Baroness Morgan, the children's minister, has issued some timely Christmas advice on how to avoid accidents in the home this Christmas. Beware exploding gravy in the microwave seems to be top of the list.

Well intentioned, I'm sure, but when you're looking for home safety advice, would a government-issue advent calendar be your first port of call? Or, as an alternative, would you perhaps use some common sense? Hmm, difficult choice...

So here are my own top tips for avoiding Christmas carnage this year:

- When cooking Christmas dinner, you will be working with boiling liquids and red-hot cooking rings or gas burners, so avoid wearing roller skates in the kitchen. This kind of footwear is more likely to make you trip and fall than good old-fashioned slippers.
- Laughter can put you at risk from an asthma attack, so try to avoid watching anything funny on the telly. Stick with repeats of *'Ello, 'Ello*, or *Last of the Summer Wine*.
- When carving the turkey, remember to remove any blindfolds that you may have been wearing during party games – knives can slice through you as easily as a turkey!
- Party-poppers are lethal weapons in the wrong hands! Always make sure a local council official has surveyed the firing area in advance of any launch. And do make sure your 'victims' are wearing British Standard safety glasses before you pull the string. Ear plugs should also be worn.
- You can avoid serious lacerations to your hands by using thick gardening gloves when opening presents – this will help prevent near-lethal paper cuts and the resulting copious loss of blood.

- Sexually-transmitted diseases are rife at this time of year, so avoid kissing Aunty Gladys on the lips when she gives you this year's *Viz* annual and half a pound of Dairy Milk – a firm shake of the hand is just as festive and refreshingly British!
- If, after Christmas lunch, you start to feel drowsy in front of the television, you're probably suffering from carbon monoxide poisoning. Don't panic! Simply get everyone out of the house, alert all your neighbours to the danger and call the police, fire brigade and ambulance service.
- If grandad wants to light up his pipe, shove him out into the garden, whatever the weather. Remember, if he smokes even one pipe or cigar in the same house as you, you will die of cancer within a month. Probably.
- Enjoy a festive drink, but don't go overboard – as a rule of thumb, when you start to feel a bit relaxed, you've already had too much and should go to the local A&E to get your stomach pumped, you filthy alcoholic!
- And remember – Christmas is a special time of year, when you and your family can enjoy some much-needed time together, as long as you can avoid murder, blood loss, deafness, industrial blindness, cancer, suffocation and scalding. And gonorrhea.

Have a wonderful, carefree Merry Christmas!

New Year resolutions

Published: December 31, 2008

In case you were wondering, the January 2009 edition of Total Politics *featured Harriet Harman dressed as Wonder Woman…*

Gordon Brown will resolve to be a bit less flippant and a bit more serious.

David Cameron will resolve to speak to his shadow Cabinet colleagues next time he uses public transport to get ~~publicity~~ to work.

Hillary Clinton will resolve to stop reminding people that the Secretary of State is fourth in line to the presidency.

Iain Dale will resolve to make ten new resolutions, numbered in order of importance.

William Hague will resolve to become an even better MP in 2009 by expanding his outside interests a bit.

Guido Fawkes will resolve to speak kindly of all in elected office and to treat them with due deference.

George Osborne will resolve to book his next holiday through Thomas Cook.

Liam Byrne will resolve to let his civil servants know, by memo, that he no longer takes sugar.

Harriet Harman will resolve to persuade Jack to remove his framed January 2009 edition of *Total Politics*.

Lord Mandelson will resolve to book his next holiday through Thomas Cook.

Barack Obama will resolve to check up where the Secretary of State is in the line of succession.

Bob Marshall-Andrews will resolve to open the big envelope that arrives each week from the Chief Whip and actually find out what that bit of pink paper is.

Alex Salmond will resolve, at last, to bin his Union Flag pants – if only they weren't so damn comfy!

Jonathan Ross will resolve to dial '141' first when making telephone calls in 2009.

Dominic Grieve will resolve to wear a bow-tie in 2009, thereby making his transition to Walter Softy complete.

David Davis will resolve to work up the courage to tell Shami about his views on capital punishment. But only when the time is right.

Damian Green will resolve to pay more attention the next time he's invited to donate to the Police Officers' Benevolent Fund.

Have a great New Year!

Unsolicited support

Published: January 5, 2009

Home Secretary Jacqui Smith's husband was reported to have written letters to his local newspapers in support of his wife, without mentioning he was married to her.

5 January 2009

Dear Prime Minister

I have never met Tom Harris and in fact have never even heard of him. Nevertheless he was an outstanding minister at the Department for Transport and I think you should reappoint him to ministerial office at the earliest opportunity. Mr Harris (of whom, let me remind you, I have never heard) is a very articulate and effective Member of Parliament who was very sympathetic to me when my husband was recently sacked from his job – or would have been sympathetic, I'm sure, had I ever met him or, indeed, heard of him.

He is also, I'm sure (though, never having met him, I can't be certain) a very good father and husband with an excellent sense of humour and wide interests outside politics. I expect he's quite the raconteur when the topic of after-dinner discussion turns to science fiction in general or *Doctor Who* in particular and I'm quite sure he's not at all boring on the subject, oh no, not at all.

So I would be grateful if you could give him another job because, frankly, he's driving his wife (whom I have also never met, heard of or about whose existence I have no firm evidence) round the bend with his constant requests that she writes anonymous supportive letters for him.

Yours

Caroline Harrison
Glasgow

Yet another leaked memo
Published: January 8, 2009

CONSERVATIVE PARTY CENTRAL OFFICE ECONOMIC ATTACK LINES FOR USE BY TORY CANDIDATES AND BLOGGERS

Action	Respose
If the Bank of England raises interest rates	'This is madness – it will make it far more difficult for businesses to borrow, and put people's mortgages up, thereby increasing the number of repossessions!'

Action	Respose
If the Bank of England lowers interest rates	'This is madness – it won't make it any easier for businesses to borrow. It's like printing money!'
If the government announces a recapitalisation of the banks	'This is an utter waste of money!'
If the government refuses to recapitalise the banks	'You're leaving customers high and dry!'
If the Chancellor announces a cut in VAT	'A gimmick!'
If the Chancellor refuses to cut VAT	'The Chancellor's refusal to give money back to shoppers is a disgrace!'
If the government announces a multi-billion pound package to boost the economy	'This is profligacy!'
If the government refuses to announce a multi-billion pound package to boost the economy	'They're just being blinkered!'
If the government nationalises Northern Rock	'This is simply a return to the '70s!'
If the government refuses to nationalise Northern Rock	'This is simply a return to the '90s!'*
If the government claims the credit crunch started in the US	'It started in the UK!'
If the government points out the downturn is as severe in the rest of Europe	'It started in the UK!'
If Iceland (the country) goes bust	'It's Gordon Brown's fault!'
If Iceland (the shop) goes bust	'It's Gordon Brown's fault!'
If Woolies goes bust	'It's Gordon Brown's fault! (And did you know that David did all his Christmas shopping there? Every bit of it, oh yes!)'**

* Still to be checked
** Still to be checked

Lib Dem reshuffle! Latest!!

Published: January 8, 2009

Traffic in every major city in the country ground to a standstill today as crowds waited with bated breath to see the result of Nick Clegg's shadow Cabinet reshuffle.

Daytime TV programming was interrupted as news emerged (the results of Dwayne's DNA results had to be postponed until tomorrow) and printing of newspapers' evening editions was delayed until the reshuffle was completed.

Apparently a bloke with glasses has been moved sideways and somebody else has kept his job. Or something.

But I'll bet the BBC's (correct) decision not to describe any of Clegg's team as 'shadow' anything will annoy them.

I know what I like

Published: February 15, 2009

The brother of a friend of mine once told his grandfather that he intended to go to art college after leaving school. The old man looked at his grandson suspiciously and replied: 'Art? That's a' done wi' computers up north!'

Not sure, but I think I know what he meant, or at least where he was coming from. Art's reputation has been tarnished in modern times; once seen as the achievement of geniuses whose skill one could only marvel at, it is now more often perceived as a confidence trick perpetrated by smart young graduates 'expressing' themselves all over the place.

I confess to being a philistine (or should that be 'Philistine'?); I don't 'get' most modern art. I apply a similar criterion to the definition of art as I do to the definition of sport. When embroiled in the familiar pub discussion about whether or not darts is a sport, I make the point that an activity should only be considered a sport if being fitter helps improve your performance. Ergo, darts is a game but not a sport. Okay, it's not a perfect rule, but it works for me.

So with the question of 'what is art?' I ask: 'Could I, as someone who has never received any training as an artist, physically produce that piece of work to the same technical standard?'

I look at an unmade bed, or a room with a light switch in it, or, at a pinch, a collection of bricks, and I have to answer 'yes, I could do that'. It may be whimsical, or represent a profound concept to the 'artist', but when I look at some of the classic paintings in Tate Britain or Kelvingrove Art Gallery, I see genius, and I marvel at how any human being could be so blessed with such an incomprehensible level of skill. I see Tracey Emin's unmade bed and I see an emperor's new clothes. Not only could I have produced that, I have done on many occasions, and not been paid for my trouble.

As I say, I'm a philistine/Philistine.

So here's my proposition: nominate this site for the Turner Prize. No, seriously.

It's innovative – how many other candidates for the prize have nominated themselves? It's interactive – you can leave a comment and the author/artist may even respond. It's about self-expression, both of the artist and of those who visit it. Visitors to the gallery could become part of the exhibit even as they viewed it (provided I was available to moderate comments at that time). It's democratic – anyone can participate.

Plus, my plugging it as a contender is itself a totally post-ironic and avant garde act: how cutting edge can anyone get, dahling?!

And, most important of all, it doesn't deserve to be nominated for, or to win, any major artistic prize. So, a sure thing, I would've said.

You can just see it, can't you, on the news reports of this year's Turner Prize shortlist: a lonely, isolated iMac sitting in the centre of a gallery in the Tate Modern. The camera pans slowly round to reveal my big baw face looking out at you. Genius, yeah?

No.

So get on the phone/web/email to the Turner Prize people and get lobbying. Now's our chance people – our chance to claim one of the art world's most prestigious prizes for the blogscape*, while exposing said prize as a delusionary irrelevance. And let's face it: what could be more irrelevant than this blog?

* © Bryan Appleyard

Print out this post and send it to at least five other people!

Published: March 2, 2009

Carolyn received this nonsense in an email over the weekend. The internet has been a Godsend to those sad individuals who used to spend every waking minute copying out chain letters by hand and sending them on to friends who, if they had any wits about them, would put them straight in the bin.

Anyway, I've annotated this one. The comments in italics are mine but the actual letter itself is, believe it or not, genuine. And I can't help thinking that there are plenty of mugs out there who take this sort of thing seriously.

Anyway – avanti!

This is without a doubt one of the nicest good luck forwards I have received. Hope it works for you – and me!
('One of the nicest good luck forwards I have received'? You mean you score them?)

Lotus Touts: You have 6 minutes

There's some mighty fine advice in these words, even if you're not superstitious. This Lotus Touts has been sent to you for good luck from the Anthony Robbins organisation. It has been sent around the world ten times so far.

(Okay, first of all: 'mighty fine'? Well, alright, li'l lady, sure is good speakin' to y'all... And who are the Anthony Robbins organisation? I'm too depressed even to Google it.)

Do not keep this message.
(Have no fear)

The Lotus Touts must leave your hands in 6 MINUTES. Otherwise you will get a very unpleasant surprise. This is true, even if you are not superstitious, agnostic, or otherwise faith impaired.
(Look, mate, first of all, this is an email – it's not in 'my hands', it's 'on my screen'. And what will be the 'unpleasant surprise'? Oh, I just worked it out: another message from the Anthony Robbins organisation.)

ONE. Give people more than they expect and do it cheerfully.
(I was giving my bank grief over the phone the other day. Neither of us was very cheerful about it, to be honest.)

TWO. Marry a man/woman you love to talk to. As you get older, their conversational skills will be as important as any other.
(Ah, you see, there's a problem: I've only ever met one man/woman. It was in a bar in Soho and he/she was perfectly pleasant, but we just never clicked. Granted, his operation would have given us something to hone our conversational skills on for a lifetime.)

THREE. Don't believe all you hear, spend all you have or sleep all you want.
(Or read all you see in an email. You forgot that one.)

FOUR. When you say, 'I love you', mean it.
(Really? Gosh, you've done a degree in this, haven't you?)

FIVE. When you say, 'I'm sorry', look the person in the eye.
(Unless you don't actually mean it, in which case just stare at your feet and mumble.)

SIX. Be engaged at least six months before you get married.
(Be engaged doing what? You mean, on the phone? That would be very expensive. Unless you're using Skype.)

SEVEN. Believe in love at first sight.
(Or, failing that, lust at first grope.)

EIGHT. Never laugh at anyone's dreams. People who don't have dreams don't have much.
(No – people who don't have much, don't have much. And what about that dream where I was on Stars in Their Eyes *– that was hilarious!)*

NINE. Love deeply and passionately. You might get hurt but it's the only way to live life completely.
(Actually, not getting hurt is miles better.)

TEN. In disagreements, fight fairly. No name calling.
(What a prat.)

ELEVEN. Don't judge people by their relatives.
(Even Jesus?)

TWELVE. Talk slowly but think quickly.
(And if you can't remember that, rub your belly and pat your head at the same time.)

THIRTEEN! When someone asks you a question you don't want to answer, smile and ask, 'Why do you want to know?'
(And then punch them in the face and run away/pretend to faint.)

FOURTEEN. Remember that great love and great achievements involve great risk.
(Especially if you're in love with the girlfriend of a mafia godfather.)

FIFTEEN. Say 'bless you' when you hear someone sneeze.

(Unless you're German, of course.)

SIXTEEN. When you lose, don't lose the lesson.
(The lesson being: don't ever lose.)

SEVENTEEN. Remember the three R's: Respect for self; Respect for others; and Responsibility for all your actions.
(That's only two Rs. Still, one more than the original three Rs, where there was one R, one W and one A.)

EIGHTEEN. Don't let a little dispute injure a great friendship.
(Absolutely – that's right, isn't it, Tony and Gordon?)

NINETEEN. When you realise you've made a mistake, take immediate steps to correct it.
(Plug in the shredder.)

TWENTY. Smile when picking up the phone. The caller will hear it in your voice
(And will assume you are a nutter.)

TWENTY-ONE. Spend some time alone.
(Something the writer of this email has quite a lot of experience in.)

Now, here's the FUN part!
(I remain unconvinced, but try me.)

Send this to at least 5 people and your life will improve.
1-4 people: Your life will improve slightly.
5-9 people: Your life will improve to your liking.
9-14 people: You will have at least 5 surprises in the next 3 weeks
15 and above: Your life will improve drastically and everything you ever dreamed of will begin to take shape.
100 or more: You will spend the rest of your life in an institution.
(Sorry, that last one should have been in italics and inside brackets.)

A true friend is someone who reaches for your hand and touches your heart. Do not keep this message.
(Ah, but you didn't say 'Don't blog it'.)

That Labour Party honesty pledge in full

Published: July 2, 2009

One of the responses to the MPs' expenses scandal was to suggest that prospective candidates sign up to pledges of one sort or another.

I'm not exactly a fan of so-called integrity pledges for political candidates. But Paul Waugh at the *Evening Standard* last week had the lowdown on the ~~pointless~~ inspired list of pledges which all Labour candidates must now sign up to.

And I've been able to get hold of the original draft...

- The Labour Party is a great movement for change, made up of people determined to serve the public interest and not their own;
- I seek elected office for the honour of serving the public and our democracy and not to use it just as a way of meeting girls;
- I will subscribe to high standards of integrity, transparency, accountability and prudence with public money – which means I will use the cheapest possible marker pens to redact my expenses;
- I will publish online my full salary and parliamentary allowances: voters can access the information if they pay a modest charge – all major credit cards accepted;
- I believe it a duty to hold regular meetings, engagement events and surgeries with my community and constituents and will do so. I also believe it's a duty not to attack constituents with large inflatable bananas but I'm forty-five years old and don't need to be told that either;

- I will communicate regularly with my electorate and will be available through email, telephone and other means to my constituents. Yes, the days when MPs used to cower behind their office doors pretending not to be in and using carrier pigeons and tin cans joined by string are at last behind us;
- I will regularly report back to my constituency party as well as to my constituents, and I will remember to follow each inhalation of oxygen with a similar sized exhalation;
- I will not use elected office to commission the building of a giant underground headquarters inside an extinct volcano from where I can launch attacks on Soviet and American spacecraft, thereby provoking a world war, or wear a safari suit, or feed my assistant to piranha fish. Probably.

Pretty much common sense, most of it.

Hold the front page!
Published: July 23, 2009

David Cameron has given a world exclusive to *The Sun*, according to *ConservativeHome*.

Hold tight for this one, folks! Because Dave has only gone and revealed…

'David Cameron tells *The Sun* he is ready to govern.'

That's completely thrown the news agenda for the day, then, hasn't it? But that's Dave for you – completely unpredictable; he's a rebel, that lad – a maverick who doesn't play by the rules, if you will.

I can imagine the moment when this devastating nugget was revealed to the editor:

Editor: *So what's Cameron saying, then? The usual stuff about not being ready to govern?*

Reporter: *Well, actually, boss, quite the opposite.*

Editor: *What do you mean?*

Reporter: *Well, he's said he's ready to govern.*

Editor: *Jesus H. Christ! You're sure?*

Reporter: *At least, that's what my notes say – my shorthand isn't what it was. But I remember doing a double-take when he said it. I was shocked!*

Editor: *Let's think straight here. Has any other paper got this?*

Reporter: *I don't think so...*

Editor: *You don't think so? You'd better be sure, because when this comes out it'll be the biggest political story since Major announced he watched Morse.*

Reporter: *Really? You think it's that big?*

Editor: *There'll be an award in this for you! Okay, tell the desk to drop that story about Madonna and Peter Andre's wedding – we've got our scoop!*

A long time ago, in a stable far, far away...
Published: December 4, 2009

Ronnie, who started his primary education this year, will be appearing in his class's nativity play soon.

He will not be playing Joseph. 'Good!' said I to his mother. 'Rubbish part. The best part is the innkeeper.'

'How so, oh wise husband of mine?' said Carolyn (okay, that's not *exactly* what she said, but you get my drift).

So why does the innkeeper play such an important part in the whole First Christmas broo-haha?

Well, remember that part where the Imperial Star Destoyer captures the rebel blockade runner in its tractor beam at the very start of *Episode IV*? And then the droids escaped to the surface of Tatooine with the Death Star tapes in the escape pod? Well, remember the Imperial gunner who almost shoots the pod down? And then he doesn't because 'there are no life forms on board'?

Well that bloke is recognised among ~~theologians~~ *Star Wars* fans everywhere as the most crucial, pivotal character in the whole original trilogy. If he had followed his original instinct and blown the escape pod to bits, then the droids wouldn't have made it to Tatooine or into the ownership of Luke Skywalker. Obi-Wan would have stayed in retirement, Uncle Owen and Aunt Beru wouldn't have been slaughtered by storm troopers and Princess Leia's execution aboard the Death Star would have gone ahead as scheduled. The Death Star's fatal weakness would not have been uncovered and would not have been destroyed, so, eventually, would have destroyed the Rebel Alliance.

All because that gunner opened fire on the escape pod. Which he didn't.

'Are you drunk?'

So, anyway, back to Bethlehem two thousand years ago. The innkeeper could easily have gone that extra mile for his last-minute customers, Mary and Joseph. He could have found a room somewhere. Or he could have sent them packing with a warning not to use his stable or else he'll get the centurions onto them. Where would the Nativity have been then?

Shepherds are rarely allowed into hotel lobbies, for a start. The Wise Men (the number of whom is not specified in Scripture) would have been hard pressed to track down the actual room number. So no Frankincense, gold or myrrh – and no tradition of prezzies at this time of year!!

Theologically speaking, the Lord being born in a manger provided a powerful message about the humility of His beginnings; a Travelodge doesn't quite have the same impact.

So, to sum up: the innkeeper's the part you want to go for, son.

'He's playing a king,' said Carolyn. 'And I fell asleep during *Star Wars*.'

Right.

Ten uses for a 'Nick Clegg'

Published: June 21, 2010

David Miliband has suggested that Nick Clegg is the Prime Minister's 'dumb waiter': 'He is not allowed to say anything, he sits there patting David Cameron on the arm during Prime Minister's Questions and then he has to serve up whatever his master decides.'

So what else is Nick Clegg for?

1. Babysitter for Dave and Sam's kids.
2. A tour guide to show Tory Cabinet ministers round Downing Street.
3. Someone to take pictures of Tory Cabinet ministers and their families outside Number 10.
4. Minute-taker at Cabinet meetings.
5. Government's Hand-Wringer-in-Chief (yes, that's a real job these days).
6. Human shield (to take the hit for the PM when Tory right-wing backbenchers chuck their rolled-up order papers at the back of Cameron's head during PMQs).
7. A coat rack.
8. An instant detoxification solution.
9. Can take confession and grant absolution. Probably.
10. He's the only member of Cameron's entourage who will agree to take Olivia Newton John's part in *Summer Nights* (to the Prime Minister's John Travolta) during Conservative HQ's occasional karaoke evenings.

Statement from Number 10: The Deputy Prime Minister

Published: July 22, 2010

Deputy Prime Minister Nick Clegg (no, I'll never get used to writing that) caused a bit of a stir by unilaterally changing the British constitution while standing in for his boss at Prime Minister's Questions, when he abandoned collective Cabinet responsibility and criticised the Iraq war as 'illegal'. Number 10 later clarified that he was speaking personally and not for the government. Which is odd, given he was doing it from the government despatch box in the Commons...

22 July 2010

The Deputy Prime Minister may have given the impression in recent months that he occasionally speaks on behalf of Her Majesty's Government and even of the Prime Minister. This impression has been encouraged by irresponsible media reporting and typical smears from the Labour Party, who have mounted a campaign of dishonesty over Nick Clegg's role in government.

This impression may also have been exacerbated through the ambiguous title Mr Clegg took for himself as soon as the coalition talks were over and before anyone else in the room could say 'bagsy' on the DPM's title. Nevertheless, he got there before Hague did, so what can you do?

But for the record, the media are instructed to ignore everything the DPM says in future, whether he says it in the Commons, in the rose garden of Number 10 or in his bath. Mr Clegg speaks only in a private capacity and nothing he says has any relation to government policy. Except for the bits where he says he loves Dave. We don't mind that.

Defending the 'police state'

Why I'll vote for 42-days

Published: May 10, 2008

*Gordon Brown had announced his intention to succeed where Tony
Blair failed and introduce pre-charge detention for terrorist suspects
for periods of up to six weeks.*

He failed, too.

Someone recently asked me why I supported government plans to
introduce a new upper limit of 42-days detention without charge.
'Because we couldn't get 90-days through,' I replied.

Smoke without fire

Published: July 7, 2008

I have no love for cigarettes. Apart from a couple of ill-judged
Camels while on holiday in Prague in 1995 (and, inevitably, a fine
Cuban on the evening of Labour's 1997 victory), I've never smoked.
My mother, who chain smoked from a very young age, died of lung
cancer a few years ago. So, as I say, not a big fan of the weed.

Having said all that, I didn't vote for the complete ban which
has been in force in England for exactly a year; I voted instead for
what was in Labour's 2005 manifesto: a ban in areas where cooked
food is served.

Nevertheless, the ban has proved more popular and workable
than I had expected, even among smokers.

Now I read of proposals to classify movies according to their
smoking content. All very well, but I do hope we're not going
to start retrospectively editing classic movies in the same way
some iconic photographs have been butchered. I remember being
appalled that a publicity shot of The Beatles had been digitally
altered to remove the band members' fags from their hands. What
next? Taking Winston Churchill's cigar away?

I was relieved to see that Sebastian Faulks, in writing the new Bond novel, had maintained his hero's addiction to tobacco. Relieved not because it's a particularly cool or attractive habit – it's not, it's pretty disgusting – but because the character Ian Fleming created was a smoker, and characters set in the 1960s shouldn't have twenty-first century standards imposed upon them retrospectively. That would be entirely dishonest. It would be the equivalent of remaking *Tess of the d'Urbervilles* and depicting Angel Clare as a feminist.

But let's get this in perspective. *Terminator 3: Rise of the Machines* featured one of the most gratuitous scenes of graphic violence I have ever seen, depicting the death of a police officer by a killer android who drives its arm through the back of his seat, through his stomach to take control of the car he's driving. And that was given a 12A certificate. Under these proposals, had Arnie lit up a fag, I'm guessing it would have been given a 15 or even an 18 certificate. Come on.

And given that two thirds of stabbings occur when the attacker has been drinking, can we expect scenes where James Bond orders a vodka martini to be cut or for the movie in question to be restricted to adults only?

Of course film producers and actors must have a responsibility to their younger, more impressionable audience members and not be complicit in their making any health-damaging lifestyle choices. But we have to draw the line at preventing young audiences watching classic movies like *Casablanca* or *Doctor No* just because the main protagonists have a taste for cigarettes.

The smack of too much government
Published: October 8, 2008

The amendment referred to in this post was never voted on and fell by default. Some commenters had queried my reference to voting against it 'if I'm still here'. A simple explanation: I had been sacked less than a week earlier and, still deeply scunnered, I had decided to head home early, daring the whips to take issue with me for missing a vote. Get me!

There may well be a vote later on today on the vexed question of whether parents should be allowed legally to smack their children.

The amendment to the Children and Young Persons Bill has been tabled by Kevin Barron MP, who also proposed the full smoking ban two years ago.

Should parents smack their children? Probably not. Are those who smack their kids child abusers or even bad parents? Not usually. Should parents who smack their children be criminalised at the stroke of a parliamentary clerk's pen? Of course not.

And should police officers' time be spent investigating the complaint of a three-year-old who's annoyed because he got a smack on the legs from his harrassed mother? Is that the best use of police resources?

Finally, is it the role of the state to raise other people's children? Of course not.

Physical chastisement isn't necessarily (or even usually) abuse. And an unenforceable law would end up being obeyed only by those who are no risk to their children and completely ignored by those who are the worst offenders.

So if we reach that particular amendment while I'm still here, I'll be voting against.

An Orwellian nightmare? Oh, wake up!
Published: October 30, 2008

An odd thing arrived today at the office: an Amazon package containing a brand new copy of *Nineteen Eighty-Four* by George Orwell. It's not the book itself that is odd – I read it for the first time nearly thirty years ago and it's a rollicking good yarn, with a great plot and a very dramatic ending.

What was peculiar was that I didn't order it from Amazon – apparently it was a gift from an anonymous benefactor. The following text was written on the packing slip:

> *Young man, this is a reminder that this book, contrary to what your leader might think, is NOT an instruction manual, but a warning. REMEMBER – WE are YOUR masters.*

Hmm. Where to start, where to start…?

Well, first of all, how about the arrogance of anyone referring to anyone else as anyone's 'masters'?

Secondly, there seem to be an awful lot of people out there – perhaps dozens of them – who seem to get strangely exercised at the prospect of a 'police state'. Except that what they define as a 'police state' is a million light years from what Orwell himself described. CCTV cameras in the street? That's just like *Nineteen Eighty-Four*, when families were monitored in their own homes, twenty-four hours a day! Can't use racist terms to vilify people anymore? Well, surely that's thought crime, just like Orwell predicted!

What rubbish. As I've written here before, this is all paranoid fantasy, and why so many people get off on it, I'll never know. I recently had the latest in a series of requests from constituents regarding CCTV. Requests to have the cameras removed? No, no, no… Requests for *more* cameras.

(Incidentally, despite a previous appeal, I still haven't been contacted by any Tory MP or candidate who has volunteered to wield the axe on any of their own local schemes. Funny, that.)

I well remember the miners' strike of 1984–85 and the claims by some on the Trotskyite left at the time that Thatcher had inaugurated a police state in her attempts to control violent picketing. And again I say: rubbish.

We live in a democracy and just because those – including my anonymous benefactor – who get excited about such things are unhappy that Labour is in power, that does not make us anything other than a democracy. And democratically-elected governments govern with the consent of the people. Yes, even this one!

While the strange person who sent me my book and others like him might claim that everyone in the UK is utterly consumed with fury over a perceived decline in civil liberties in this country, the facts are that we still enjoy a level of freedom that maintains our position as one of the great democracies of the world.

Now, if you'll excuse me, I'm going to duck now...

UPDATE at 3.07 pm: It seems my objection to the term 'masters' is causing some annoyance. For the avoidance of doubt, I regard my constituents as 'employers' rather than 'masters', fellow citizens to whom I am accountable. But 'masters' is *so* eighteenth century, don't you think?

Postal vote applications likely to increase
Published: April 9, 2009

Let's get one thing straight: the government does not want to give prisoners the right to vote.

That's the kind of thing the Lib Dems would do voluntarily; but it looks like the government will have to concede the principle against its better judgment, following an absurd ruling by the European Court of Human Rights.

Prisoners sentenced to less than four years in prison may be enfranchised, following a government consultation on how we plan to respect the European court ruling.

But before you rush to your keyboard to type out inevitable words like 'typical', 'NuLiebore', 'referendum' and 'Lisbon Treaty', can I draw your attention to the remarks by Dominic Grieve, the shadow Justice Secretary:

'The principle that those who are in custody after conviction should not have the opportunity to vote is a perfectly rational one.

Civic rights go with civic responsibility, but these rights have been flagrantly violated by those who have committed imprisonable offences.

The government must allow a parliamentary debate which gives MPs the opportunity to insist on retaining our existing practice that convicted prisoners can't vote.'

Interestingly, at no point does he suggest that a future Tory government would do anything different from us. All he's doing is stating the blindingly obvious ('Civic rights go with civic responsibility, but these rights have been flagrantly violated by those who have committed imprisonable offences') to try to persuade voters that with him in office the policy would change, without actually saying that. Because, as a good lawyer (and he *is* a good lawyer, incidentally) he knows that if the Tories ever do form a government in the future, they'll have to comply with the European Court as well.

But there's an interesting post script to all this: Many readers of this blog who are not – how can I phrase this? – instinctively pro-European will want the government to ignore this ruling. I have some sympathy with that.

But the same people are likely to insist that the government *doesn't* ignore a previous ruling that it should destroy the DNA samples taken by police from those who have been arrested but who were subsequently not charged or convicted with an offence.

Complicated, this modern life business, ain't it...?

The DNA database: my struggle
Published: August 22, 2009

The European Court of Human Rights has ruled that two British men should not have had their DNA and fingerprints retained by police. Damian Green, the shadow Home Affairs minister, having had a dramatic and high profile brush with the law over his alleged receiving of government leaks, was determined to cut the DNA database down to size.

Like Damian Green MP, I'm having my own battle over the DNA database.

Hundreds of thousands of people not charged or convicted of any crime have nevertheless had their DNA taken by the police and stored, despite a European court ruling that 'innocent' people's DNA shouldn't be held.

So here's my problem: how do I persuade the police to store my DNA? Why should I, an 'innocent' person, be denied the right to have my fingerprint and other personal data included in the national database with everyone else's, 'innocent' and guilty alike?

I feel like my civil liberties are being compromised the longer this outrage continues.

Animal Farm: a lovely children's fairy tale
Published: September 13, 2009

I might as well endear myself to the ~~salivating anoraks~~ Libertarians even further by welcoming in advance the gift of a copy of *Animal Farm* by George Orwell.

When I described *Nineteen Eighty-Four* as 'a rollicking good read' after receiving a copy from Old Holborn in the post last year, I provoked a deluge of indignation. Now, so I'm told, he's preparing to send me a copy of *Animal Farm* (you know – the one you read for your O-levels if you don't have time to read *Nineteen Eighty-Four*).

Which is great news. I have a very old copy and it's always nice to get a new replacement. I might even read it again.

I've always been amazed that Disney never adapted it. Admittedly, it's a bit depressing for a fairy tale, but so was the original version of *The Little Mermaid* before the kingdom of the mouse lightened it up a bit. All you'd need is a few good tunes:

'You got four legs and he's got two, let's work together and we'll see this through...' Or how about *'I'm more equal than you, he's more equal than me, everyone's equaller than everyone else, just leave the math to me!'* And who can forget the tear-jerking *'So long Boxer, goodbye old friend, just because it's a glue factory doesn't mean it's the end...'*

Roll on November 5th.

But seriously

Conscience and judgment

Published: May 13, 2008

The Human Fertilisation and Embryology Bill was given its second reading in the Commons tonight by a big majority. Although abortion isn't yet part of the Bill, MPs will table amendments reducing the upper limit at which a woman can get an abortion, from the current twenty-four weeks to twenty-two or even twenty.

I genuinely don't know how to vote on this. Years ago when I was still an evangelical Christian*, I was a dyed-in-the-wool pro-lifer. The first – and only – time I took part in a debate at my school's debating society was to support the case against abortion. At the first Labour Party branch meeting I ever attended, I spoke against a motion which called for Labour MPs to be whipped to support the party's policy of 'abortion-on-demand'. I lost the vote and was not a popular new member.

Since then I've changed my mind. The idea of making abortion illegal repels me. I also don't think a woman should have to get the permission of two GPs in order to be 'approved' for a legal procedure. And I accept recent scientific advice that the survival rate of premature babies has not measurably improved since the current legislation was framed.

What worries me is the question: was the twenty-four-weeks limit right when it was introduced? Should it have been twenty-two or twenty weeks even then?

I don't know. I'll think and read about this more between now and the vote. There seems to have developed a consensus among Labour colleagues at least that we shouldn't tamper with legislation that was hard-won and seems to be working effectively. Colleagues whose views I deeply respect will vote for the status quo. A lobbying operation is underway and in the voting lobby tonight I was targeted by a colleague who, when I told her I hadn't yet made up my mind, wrote something indecipherable in a box next to my name.

It's a classic head vs heart thing. There's no doubt that being a parent of young children has affected my view on this. And by that I absolutely don't mean to suggest that unless you're a parent you're not qualified to make your own judgment. It's just that it is an emotional subject, as are children.

I hate the hard decisions. But as I've said before, MPs are there to make tough decisions, not easy ones. And I want to make the right one, not necessarily the one that will make me popular. Of course, whatever I do, I'll be more unpopular with some.

*I still consider myself a Christian, just not a particularly evangelical one. Chris Bryant has dubbed me a 'recovering evangelical', which I rather like.

Why must we demonise our opponents in this debate?
Published: May 19, 2008

Jackie Ashley in today's *Guardian* portrays the argument on abortion as being one between progressive liberalism and the forces of religious zealotry. What irks me as much as the dogmatic short-sightedness of the latter is the smug arrogance of the former. In a private conversation three years ago with arch pro-choice MP Dr Evan Harris, he told me: 'I expect you would deny IVF treatment to a woman who had terminal cancer?' Well, duh. It was only afterwards that I realised he was being critical!

I'm a Christian, so I suppose I'm vulnerable to the accusation that I'm allowing religious dogma to dictate how I vote tomorrow. That's not the case. I'm trying to make an objective judgement based on science and, yes, morality. Why is it that if someone feels the number of abortions that take place in this country is too high, he or she is accused of being a misogynist?

Regional variations in lesbianism

Published: May 20, 2008

It's a pity that none of the lobby journalists appeared to be in the gallery during the exchange between Geraldine Smith, the Morecambe MP, and Chris Bryant, MP for Rhondda. Challenging Geraldine's support for Iain Duncan Smith's amendment to the Bill on the basis that it would discriminate against same-sex couples, Chris suggested Geraldine had not sought the opinions of lesbians in her constituency. She replied (and this is subject to correction by Hansard): 'Actually I talk to lots of lesbians in my constituency. Maybe lesbians in Lancashire are just more down to earth than lesbians in the Rhondda.' Fantastic!

When was the last time you heard an exchange like that in the Commons? In fact, when did you last see a title like this for a blog post?

Playing God? No, just doing what He won't

Published: November 12, 2008

The awful case of 'Baby P', who died at the hands of the monsters in whose care Haringey Social Services had entrusted him, shocked the whole country. From a personal point of view, I have never felt such sadness, rage and frustration. The apologist tone of some on the Left – essentially claiming that the dead boy's 'mother' and her partner were themselves 'victims' of social exclusion – appalled me and only served to emphasise how removed I was beginning to feel from some in my party.

I genuinely don't understand the pressures that social work services are under. The case of 'Baby P' in Haringey is so distressing and awful I find it hard even to watch any of the news reports. But I know that social workers are often in an impossible position – damned if they do, damned if they don't.

Having said that, there can surely be no excuses for the appalling failure of care in this case. And I am left asking the same question that I always ask whenever such a case emerges: why aren't very young children living in threatening situations taken permanently into care and adopted to caring, loving couples?

There are certainly plenty of such couples, childless for one reason or another, who could offer these tragic children the love and protection to which they have a right. So am I wrong in assuming that social workers tend to give the benefit of the doubt to biological parents in such cases? I ask this as a genuine query, because this isn't an area I'm remotely expert in. Someone who physically abuses a child, or who allows someone else to physically abuse their child, or who is leading a chaotic lifestyle as a result of drug use, has no moral right to continue to be that child's parent, and any legal rights to be a parent must surely come under scrutiny.

When I worked as a press officer for Strathclyde Regional Council, the social work department came in for a huge amount of criticism from the media when it removed a baby from a family in Glasgow's west end and adopted the child to a couple living in another part of the region. How dare social workers play God? screamed the front pages. Return the child to its proper home, they demanded.

Having learned of some of the appalling circumstances of the case, I felt this was one of the few occasions when social workers had undoubtedly done a good thing, the right thing. The real tragedy was that the biological parents were allowed to retain care of their older children.

Baby P was in the care of brutal, evil monsters, one of whom happened to be his biological mother. No doubt there are those who will offer apologia on their behalf: they were ill-educated, poor, socially excluded. Undoubtedly there was drug or alcohol misuse involved.

I don't care. They have no excuses for their monstrous behaviour. Whatever punishment they have to endure, it cannot be enough.

Social workers playing God? With all respect to the Almighty, it was He who decided that children can be born to, and be in the care of, witless imbeciles barely capable of looking after themselves, let alone a vulnerable child. If social workers choose to remove such children – permanently – from such a situation, then they would not be playing God: they would be doing a far, far better job.

No title

Published: November 17, 2008

I was too upset to compose a title to this.

Why do I, an MP and a blogger, continue to want to write about the Baby P case, when all that happens is that I become angrier and sadder, and feel more unable actually to achieve anything positive, with every word I write?

That's the question I've been asking myself tonight as I've re-read the Executive Summary of Haringey Local Safeguarding Children Board Serious Case Review (in which, confusingly, the victim is referred to as 'Child A').

And here's what I've concluded: it's okay to get angry at the people who killed this innocent child. It's okay to hate them for the terrible injuries they inflicted on him. It's fine – I would suggest it's even desirable – to want them to suffer in turn, to seek revenge, not just justice, against these sub-humans who once lived among us and, infuriatingly, will do so again one day.

Because when a child has already been tortured and killed by the deliberate actions of those who were entrusted to care for him, then hate for them is all that's left.

Christians are supposed to forgive, to turn the other cheek, to love and never to hate.

Well, here's a confession: I'm not a very good Christian. I've always been rubbish at it, which is why I've flitted in and out of church for the last twenty-eight years.

And whatever God and the Bible says, here's what I say: sometimes it's good to hate. Sometimes it diminishes the worth of a victim by offering forgiveness to his killers. Sometimes people don't deserve forgiveness. Sometimes they deserve to suffer. And when those circumstances arise, it is utterly maddening to know for certain that our justice system, our society, will not insist that they suffer as they deserve.

And before you start praying for my soul or worrying for my state of mental health, I know the difference between emotion and logic; I understand the need for politicians and law-makers to take a step back and to bite their tongues, to bite back the bile and to make the right decision, even when it feels like the wrong one.

So Baby P's 'mother' and her awful henchmen will be punished, though not for the murder they undoubtedly committed. Some lesser charge has sufficed because lawyers have pointed out that no court could say for sure which of the culprits dealt the killing blow.

Good for them.

No similar case has affected me in quite this way, so accept my apologies for the rant. I needed to get it off my chest. In fact, I had planned to write a post about the afore-mentioned executive summary. But it's getting late and, as I said, I feel too angry, too sad and too tired to write any more.

I'll go to bed now and hope I can wash my mind of that awful image of a 17-month-old child with a shaved head and with chocolate smeared over his face by his 'mother' to hide the marks left by his attackers to ensure the attacks could continue unhindered by the authorities.

And, inevitably, now that we know of his fate a few short days after that photograph was taken, I dread what I see as the sorrow and reproach in his young eyes.

I hope we are all haunted, just a bit, by that picture. Baby P deserves that much justice, at least.

IDS may well have some answers on asylum

Published: December 15, 2008

People seem to have a lot more time for Iain Duncan Smith now than they ever did while he was Conservative leader.

This morning, for instance, he was on the *Today* programme talking about the new report by his think tank, the Centre for Social Justice, into the asylum system. He made a number of good points and I'm going to have to get a copy.

As a Glasgow MP, I have always had to deal with a large number of asylum cases. Glasgow was the only local authority in Scotland to volunteer to be part of the Home Office's asylum seeker dispersal programme, aimed at encouraging areas other than London to share responsibility for supporting asylum seekers.

In the past seven years I have gained a reputation of being hardline on the issue. If someone applies for asylum and that application is approved, they should be welcomed with open arms. If rejected, they should return to their home country. There is no doubt in my mind that the asylum system is being used more by those wishing – for perfectly understandable reasons – to come to the UK to improve the standard of living for themselves and their families, than by those genuinely in need of refuge from an oppressive state.

On more occasions than I care to remember, I have been approached by asylum seekers who tell me, at our first meeting, that despite being in the UK for six or seven years, they still haven't received a response to their initial application. What they mean is that they still haven't received a *positive* decision to their numerous appeals against the initial rejection.

If you're single and have no children, you lose your state support once you've exhausted your appeal rights. Families continue to get support until they leave – voluntarily or involuntarily. But voluntary repatriations don't happen as frequently as necessary, and involuntary removals of families – leading, occasionally, to the so-called 'dawn raids' – aren't exactly ideal levers for enforcing policy.

Even after early day removals are carried out, courts often delay or prevent a family's actual removal if a judicial review is lodged at the last minute. And JRs are almost always lodged at the very last minute. This kind of circumstance is distressing for the family, frustrating for immigration and police officers and politically difficult for MPs and the government. Surely, any new policy initiative that would make the initial application for refugee status more robust – and therefore less vulnerable to being subsequently overturned on appeal – should be considered?

IDS has thought carefully about this issue because it is an important one. He has resisted the temptation to parrot the *Daily Mail* dog whistle line of 'send them all back and the sooner the better' and has opted instead for some measured and considered analysis.

I hope the government is listening.

'Good news: we got it wrong on climate change!'
Published: January 25, 2009

Fraser Nelson has actually written something that I don't think is completely bonkers: namely that some green activists will be delighted by the drop in consumption and productivity – and, of course, the number of people in work – caused by the recession.

This is a point I made in a speech on Heathrow back in October. George Monbiot has written in eager anticipation of the downturn in an article entitled 'Bring on the recession'. Strange how people who would normally express concerns about the economic plight of people living in the Third World are now more concerned that the same Third World citizens are becoming richer (A Good Thing) and are therefore demanding a higher quality of life (Another Good Thing).

But let me paint you a picture: imagine if the Intergovernmental Panel on Climate Change announced tomorrow that 'we got it wrong – climate change isn't caused by man. Sorry about that. As you were.' (Now, I know that won't happen because the IPCC were right, but bear with me here, okay?)

What would your reaction be? I know what mine would be: delight. I'd be celebrating. I'd be popping the champagne. Celebrations tempered, of course, by the realisation that global warming is something we can't affect and we'll just have to deal with. But such an announcement would be good news, yes?

Well, no, not for some (probably a minority of) environmentalists. Because for them, the fight against global warming has another aim: the defeat of capitalism, of economic growth, of prosperity.

Which is why I find their arguments so nauseating. It must be lovely to be a high-profile journalist whose own income is high and reasonably secure. And it must be so easy to offer to sacrifice the jobs and the livelihoods of millions of working people for the good of the environment.

But unless we can find a way of saving the planet without sacrificing prosperity – here and in developing countries – then the fight is already lost.

Some of my best friends…
Published: January 27, 2009

While some parliamentary colleagues think nothing of voting against the Labour whip, for me it is a weapon of last resort and never done lightly. This post was the start of the run-up to my first rebellion…

In polite society, any debate about minorities, whether black or Asian people, homosexuals or (particularly in the west of Scotland) Roman Catholics, usually includes a sentence along the lines of 'some of my best friends are…'

So before I say something mildly controversial and off-message, let me lay my pro-gay credentials on the table.

I have always voted in the Commons for 'gay-friendly' legislation, including civil partnerships, which I'm particularly proud of. A surprisingly large number of my closest friends when I was growing up in Ayrshire turned out to be gay. The best man at my wedding is gay and his partner regularly babysits for us.

So, to sum up: Tom Harris = not remotely homophobic. Got that? Good.

I also have a lot of Christian friends, one of whom writes the GadgetVicar blog. It does seem to me that the government's plans to protect gay people from incitement to hatred might actually criminalise people like the Rev. David McCarthy, whose views on homosexuality I disagree with, but are well thought out and based on his interpretation of Scripture.

This is the amendment proposed to the legislation by Lord Waddington:

'For the avoidance of doubt, the discussion or criticism of sexual conduct or practices or the urging of persons to refrain from or modify such conduct or practices shall not be taken of itself to be threatening or intended to stir up hatred.'

Try as I might, I can see nothing there with which to disagree. If someone with too much time on his hands wants to distribute tracts to the general public advising people to desist from homosexual acts for religious reasons, that's up to him. But he should be humoured – mocked, even – but surely not prosecuted?

The nutjobs who demonstrate at the funerals of US troops killed in Iraq and Afghanistan holding placards which declare: 'God hates fags' are revolting to any sane person. But they're tolerated – by US law, if not by the many understandably infuriated members of the public who have been known to attack them.

Of course gay people deserve protection from those who would incite violence against them. But neither they nor I have any right to expect the law to protect them from being offended.

These are thoughts I've been mulling over for some time, but they were crystalised in far more eloquent form this morning by Graeme Archer at *ConservativeHome*.

Hat-tip to Iain Dale.

It's not God vs science; it's sliderule vs the Bible

Published: February 9, 2009

Thursday will mark the 200th anniversary of the birth of Charles Darwin. It is a matter of profound disappointment on my part that the celebration of the achievements of such a great man is being overshadowed (albeit only marginally) by creationists.

Much has been made of the recent survey which showed, apparently, that everyone thinks God created the universe in six days, from about the 3rd to the 9th of October 6, 118 years ago. On a Wednesday. Or something.

Now, given that similar proportions of the Great British Public also believe that Princess Diana was murdered, that the moon landings were faked and that 9/11 was mostly special effects (seriously – that is actually a 'genuine' conspiracy theory), I won't lose too much sleep over it. Creationism is just the latest silly fad that's been imported from America and one day it will fade away, just as previous fads – hula hoops, *Baywatch* and David Blaine, for example – have done.

Even for Christians, the literal truth, or otherwise, of the book of Genesis has no bearing on our faith. Or it shouldn't have. Too often, a blind and unthinking adherence to this particular dogma is simply a way of establishing their assumed superiority over other Christians: 'I'm courageous enough to believe in the literal interpretation of the Bible, against all social convention and scientific fact. That means my faith is stronger than yours.' Or words to that effect. It's the sin of pride (which, to many evangelical Christians I know, isn't nearly as serious as any other sin involving sex).

As a student, my first (and only) Christian Union meeting was sullied by a meeting with an older student who was a member of an Elim Pentecostal Church and who was very loud and arrogant in his promotion of his own views, which included creationism. I had never met anyone like this before and I was fascinated, much as Victorians were fascinated and unnerved by travelling freak shows. At one point he said that Christians shouldn't watch TV or listen to music unless it was Christian music. 'But what about Genesis?' I asked in an ill-judged attempt at levity.

'Love the book, hate the band,' replied Mark (for thus was he named).

You can imagine it was quite a swinging night. I never returned to the Christian Union and, thankfully, never came across old Mark again. But a couple of years later I found myself, as a student journalist, attending a public lecture by an American scientist who, as a Christian, had revisited the science of evolution and found it wanting. He put up quite a plausible case, I seem to remember, but I left unconvinced. My view then, as now, was 'Why does this matter to you so much that you've got to tell other people?'

Christianity is about faith, but it's primarily about an individual's relationship with God. If that relationship is stronger for believing in the literal truth of the whole Bible, well, knock yourself out, mate. But most people don't need to believe in six-day creation to have faith in God.

As for the science, I've written on this site before that evolution remains a theory, not a fact, though it remains the most plausible scientific theory on offer to explain the development of life on this particular, small planet. Our good friend, Stewart Cowan, insists that his own arguments in favour of creationism are scientifically-based.

Two important points: if your interpretation of science is founded on faith, then no amount of empirical evidence to the contrary will ever change your mind.

Secondly, if a scientist had absolutely no knowledge whatever of any of the main religions' creation stories, he would not, under any circumstances, conclude that the earth was a few thousand years old. That conclusion, in creationists' minds, is reached first, with the appropriate 'scientific' data subsequently arranged in a reverse process to justify the conclusion they want to reach.

Darwin's life and work should be celebrated. It's quite possible that much of his research and conclusions will be overtaken one day by other scientists with access to more information and resources than Darwin had. But his work remains the most solid foundation on which to base further expansion of our knowledge of the origin and development of species.

When it comes to matters of faith, the Bible can't be beaten.

When it comes to science, I will trust the judgement of someone who prefers a sliderule over a Bible every time.

Complaints: the latest alternative to debate
Published: March 11, 2009

The Advertising Standards Authority (ASA) has received more than 1,000 complaints about the Christian party's 'There is definitely a God' advertising campaign.

Some of the complainers have claimed that the ad was 'offensive' to atheists, although I guess the decision by the ASA not to launch an investigation indicates that that claim was treated with the seriousness it deserved. My, you must be a delicate little flower indeed if the mere affirmation of faith by others is 'offensive' to you!

I don't believe for a second that a single atheist was remotely offended, and even if that were the case, it's hardly a reason to ban an advert. Unfortunately, what seems to be happening is that individuals and organisations are using complaints procedures, not necessarily to maintain standards of decency or whatever, but to stymie an opposing point of view.

Politicians are at it too. In the past, any MP accused of dodgy practices could be exposed to the media glare and held to account. Now, if you don't like a particular public figure, make a complaint to the police. Yes, it will waste police time and resources, but you'll get a headline or two out of it and it's not as if the police have got anything better to do (oh, and it's also useful to have at least a shadow of an actual complaint to level against him).

I don't suppose New Scotland Yard are entirely enthusiastic about being drawn into political fights in this way. But if a complaint is made then obviously they have to act upon it.

I just can't shake the feeling that some recent complaints have been mischievous at best and vexatious at worst.

Just like the complaints against the Christian party ads.

The ruling by the ASA, although the right one, concerns me. It said that the ad fell outside its remit because it was election material. Does that mean that if a non-party political organisation – a church, for instance – wanted to proclaim the Gospel along the lines of: 'For God so loved the world that He gave His only Son so that all who believe in him shall not perish but have everlasting life', then that would be investigated on the grounds that the church could not substantiate the claims behind that statement?

Not in my name
Published: August 20, 2009

Would Thomas Hamilton, who murdered sixteen children and their teacher in a primary school in Dunblane thirteen years ago, have been released from jail on compassionate grounds had he (a) lived to be convicted and (b) developed terminal cancer?

Most people, including the Scottish justice minister, Kenny MacAskill, would, I hope, dismiss such a notion. And yet, in December 1988, Abdelbaset Ali al-Megrahi not only murdered *seventeen* children under the age of sixteen, but also 253 others. In cold blood. Without mercy. Without compassion. Without humanity.

And tonight he is flying home to the bosom of his loving and (I assume) forgiving family in Libya.

Al-Megrahi has, we are told, just three months to live. Not long, you might think. And yet for two of his victims, that is more than a lifetime: Jonathan Thomas of Southfield, Michigan, and Brittany Williams of Crown Point, New York, were each just two months old when Al-Megrahi's task of 21 December 1988 was completed successfully with the explosion in mid-air of Pan Am Flight 103 above a previously unheard-of Scottish town.

Some may argue that the lives of child murder victims are no more precious than those of any others, and I simply use Al-Megrahi's child victims to illustrate a point: why was he considered for compassionate release when others whose crimes were, arguably, less (in quantative terms only; not in relation to the devastation caused to victims' families) would almost certainly not be?

MacAskill told reporters today: 'I can only base my decision on the medical advice I have before me.' That was a false statement. If it were true, then he would not have been asked to make a decision in the first place. If the 'only' basis for a decision was Al-Megrahi's medical condition, then his release was inevitable, since the medical evidence seems to be incontrovertible. But MacAskill was asked to make a decision, a decision that had to be based on a lot more than 'the medical advice I have before me'.

He had to take into account whether or not justice would be served by the mass murderer's release. Before he became an MSP and then justice minister in the SNP government, MacAskill was a defence solicitor. His liberal instincts which allow him to sympathise with the perpetrators, rather than the victims of crime, have not let him down today.

I can't shake the feeling that not far beneath the surface of this debate has been an assumption – and if not an assumption, then certainly a suspicion – that Al-Megrahi is innocent of the crime of which he was convicted eight years ago. Yet even if this were the case, MacAskill's decision was still the wrong one. The deal (unofficially) offered to the terrorist by the Scottish government was that in order to qualify for compassionate release, he had to drop his existing appeal against his conviction. There is a widespread and near unanimous view among the families of the victims of Lockerbie that had the appeal gone ahead, it would have unearthed previously unseen evidence that could have helped answer some of the many unanswered questions surrounding the tragedy.

Thanks to MacAskill's intervention, that will now no longer happen. In his embarrassing and unsuccessful attempts to look and sound statesmanlike today, MacAskill tried to claim 'humanity' as a peculiarly Scottish characteristic. But it is too late for him to try to claim the moral high ground. This decision was made not by a minister representing the Scottish nation, but by a lawyer representing the minority Scottish government.

His decision today was wrong on the grounds of justice and wrong on the grounds of humanity. But as long as Mr MacAskill can reassure himself that it was the right decision medically, then I'm sure he'll be able to sleep as soundly tonight as Al-Megrahi will when he arrives home after a long but safe and comfortable flight.

Abusive parents have no right to care for their children
Published: September 6, 2009

Today's front page splash in *The Observer* was music to my ears: 'Take more babies away from bad parents, says Barnardo's chief'.

While I can understand the tremendous pressures that social workers are under when it comes to such decisions, I have never been able to understand the views of those who assume that children – especially very young children – are always better off with their natural parents. The priority should be 'supporting' families 'in difficulty', we are told.

'Supporting', as far as I know, means chucking limitless amounts of council tax-payers' money, in the form of social workers and related services, at dysfunctional families who, at best, are utterly incapable of providing the love and support to which every child has a right and who, at worst, regularly abuse or neglect their children, using their addiction to drugs/alcohol as an excuse.

Our, and the media's, attention is too often focused exclusively on those dramatic and heartbreaking cases such as Baby P. But just because many of the kids living with abusive, uncaring, unloving parents manage to survive until they're old enough to come under the purview of the police rather than the social services does not mean that intervention – sorry, 'support' – has been successful.

If social services intervention results in the long-term low-level abuse and neglect by its natural parents, then that is a tragedy.

Parenthood is a privilege, not a right. If you can't do it properly, don't do it at all. The adults who are responsible for the heart-wrenching misery of their offspring have had their chance. They're adults, they can make choices for themselves. Their children can't, and should be rescued from their abusers at as early a point as possible. Not only would it result in happy children being loved by their adoptive parents throughout their lives, it would save a colossal amount of public money, which is currently being poured down the drain marked 'intervention'.

UPDATE at 10.52am on Monday 7 September: My assertion that parenthood is a privilege, not a right, seems to have caused some apoplexy on both right and left (which is how I like it). But a right is something that can be enforced in law, through the court system if necessary. If a couple find themselves unable physically to have a child, the state may choose to offer IVF treatment, but the couple have no right to a successful course of treatment, and have no recourse to law if they remain infertile. Similarly, if a mother has her child taken away from her because she is too drug-addled to care properly for the child, which of her rights is being violated? None. As Benjamin Gray said on this thread: 'The child has rights, the parent duties.'

Success! In your face, atheists!
Published: December 16, 2009

I've been banging on for a while now, in a very *Daily Mail* kind of way, about the loss of the word 'Christmas' from various local authorities' official celebrations.

I accept there's a lot of misinformation and exaggeration about this. But I also know that in Glasgow, the council have been promoting 'Winterfest' for a few years now. No one really knows why. No one ever steps forward to defend such nonsense because there isn't actually any kind of cogent argument against calling Christmas 'Christmas' or against recognising that, however you celebrate it (or even if you don't celebrate it at all) it is an important event in the Christian calendar, marking the birth of Jesus Christ, the Son of God.

So this year, I decided to express my frustration with this practice by writing to the leader of Glasgow City Council, Steven Purcell.

He has replied:

> (Winterfest) was picked not to hide Christmas or to avoid giving offence but to reflect the fact that there are events in (George) square that are not connected to Christmas such as the St Andrew's Day celebrations and Hogmanay.

> My personal view is that this has not been particularly successful and so from next year we will no longer use the phrase Winterfest in our marketing.

So, job done. And I understand that, although no final decision has been taken about what to call 'Christmas' in Glasgow next year, it will at least feature the word 'Christmas'.

So, for the very last time: a very merry Winterfest to you all...

Now, all I have to do is convince Steven to do something about the ugly Christmas mess that George Square has become.

Sixty is too old to be a mum
Published: January 19, 2010

Sue Tollefson is fifty-nine years old. She gave birth for the first time twenty-two months ago and, with more help from a foreign-based IVF clinic, she hopes to have another.

So will you say it, or shall I? Oh, alright then... What a selfish woman.

Apparently, there's a debate taking place in Britain about whether sixty is too old to become a mum. What a depressing thought. There has to be a debate about it? Why? Are we really so stupid and shallow that we need a debate before we reach the obvious conclusion of 'Yes, of course sixty is too old to become a mum'?

Mrs Tollefsen, told *The Sun*: 'Every woman has a right to be a mother.' No, they don't. Having a child, becoming a parent is a privilege, not a right.

That is, of course, easy for someone who is already the proud father of three boys to say. I agree that it's not fair that some women who desperately want to have children reach the age when they can collect their pension but still haven't achieved that ambition.

But what's even more unfair is knowing that a child is born with the near certainty of being left motherless before it reaches its teens, or will spend their formative years as a carer.

Children are not lifestyle choices. They're not possessions to be added to our collections of material wealth as we grow older: first car (used), first flat, first house, second car (new), baby, bigger house... Children are precious for their own sake. The happiness and fulfilment they offer to their parents is secondary.

'But no one says that a 60-year-old man is too old to have a baby,' say Mrs Tollefsen's supporters. Well, actually, I think sixty is too old for anyone to become a parent. But to use drugs to fool a body into thinking it is young enough to be fertile is plain wrong. There is a very good reason why nature, in its wisdom, decided that women should face a cut-off point after which they can no longer conceive: it makes it far more likely that when a baby is born, one parent or another will be around long enough to look after it.

The only up side to this story is that Mrs Tollefsen had to go to Russia to receive this treatment because she wouldn't have received it in the UK. I wish the same could be said for every country. There are those who are so wedded to the concept of 'rights' for everyone (except the rights of infants, obviously) that they will campaign for such treatment to become available here also.

They must be opposed. That will be heartbreaking for many older childless women. But it is fairer to children, and in this equation, that's all that matters.

Foreign affairs

When 'terrorism' isn't terrorism

Published: September 2, 2008

Conspiracy theories and the strange individuals who waste their time reading about them can be easily dispensed with. What is more dangerous are those who seek to use their status, position and skills to justify or excuse acts of terrorism.

A few years back I was greatly offended by an article in *The New Statesman* by John Pilger. No surprise there, you might say – wasn't everyone? Pilger had written a piece about 9/11 and had come out with all the usual nonsense about how America wasn't really the victim. What incensed me was his use of the word 'terrorists' to describe Muhammad Atta and his fellow murderers. Let me make this clear: Pilger inserted inverted commas around the word 'terrorist' within his article.

Now, my understanding of journalistic rules is that there are two reasons for using double inverted commas: when quoting someone, and to indicate irony. Pilger was not quoting anyone, so he was using 'terrorist' as an ironic description of the ... er, terrorists.

The implication Pilger intended was that Atta and his henchmen were unfairly labelled as terrorists by the mainstream media, but that he wasn't going to make the same mistake, oh no. After all, anyone who hated the United States that much can't be all bad, surely?

I found myself writing a letter of complaint, which was published and, surprisingly, responded to by Pilger himself. Can't remember now what names he called me; they probably weren't any worse than some of the things left as comments on this blog.

We should be very careful indeed of those in the mainstream media using language that seeks, even in a subtle way, to excuse or justify acts of random murder. Explain, yes; excuse, never.

An Iraq inquiry will change nothing

Published: December 20, 2008

According to TheyWorkForYou, I voted 'strongly against' an inquiry into the war in Iraq. Apparently.

Now that a date has been set for withdrawal of British troops from Iraq, an inquiry is back on the agenda. But an inquiry into what? Nick Clegg says he wants an inquiry into 'an illegal war'. So, no prejudging the outcome there, then.

And if Nick doesn't think the legality or otherwise of the war needs to be looked at, what does he want to be examined? An inquiry into the conduct of the war, or of events leading up to the start of the war, would be fair enough. But I would not support an inquiry seeking to make judgements about political decisions made in February and March 2003 by ministers and MPs. Yes, MPs sometimes make mistakes and, when that occurs, they are responsible for those misjudgements to their electorates, not to an inquiry headed up by some judge or other who isn't accountable to anyone.

Similarly, ministers should be responsible to Parliament, not to an inquiry. Supposing Judge Whoever decides that the decision to go to war should not have been made. He or she is entitled to his or her view. But my judgement, and the judgement of most MPs, was that it should. The electorate have since had an opportunity to make their own judgement.

Whenever an inquiry is held, and whatever its structure, it will be a huge disappointment to many people. Many of those calling for an inquiry are doing so only because they expect it will bolster their own view on Iraq.

But I doubt if there is a single person in the UK (among those who care one way or the other) whose mind is not already made up about the justification, or lack of it, for the invasion of Iraq. Personally, I'm not about to change my mind just because an inquiry tells me I should. And before you start fulminating at my arrogance, just remember that the same goes for those who opposed, and still oppose, the occupation: will any of them change their mind if the inquiry concludes the invasion was justified? Of course not.

An inquiry will happen; an inquiry *should* happen. Just don't expect it to draw a line under this particular episode.

Iraq

Published: January 31, 2009

I recommend the interview with Tony Blair in today's *Times*.

Inevitably, the consequent coverage I've seen focuses on our former Prime Minister's feelings about his legacy with specific regard to Iraq. His response?

> I'm not haunted by it, but of course I reflect on it, and am troubled by it, and feel a great sense of responsibility for it. Of course I do.

Many friends who enthusiastically supported Labour in 1997 and 2001, feel very little but contempt for Blair because of Iraq. It's like the old joke about the man who has many accomplishments to his name: 'But what am I best known for?' he asks indignantly. 'One sheep, one sodding sheep...'

Even now, nearly six years after the two crucial Commons votes that led us to invasion, war and occupation, Iraq remains, for many, the single biggest mistake committed by Labour during its twelve years in office. And as you would expect, as one of those MPs who supported the government on both votes, I'm often asked: why?

Within the question there is often an assumption that those of us who voted for war had the same single-minded conviction as those who opposed it. And it's true that many who voted for the war did in fact have an absence of doubt that was shared by their opponents. I envied them, for I did not, and I still don't.

I simply couldn't comprehend how any MP could walk into either division lobby on such a controversial and complex issue without a glimmer of doubt in his mind, whichever lobby he was walking into. For my part, I wrestled long and hard with the various arguments, changing my mind a dozen times about how I intended to vote. Those who marched against the war, who now hate everything about Labour and Tony Blair because their protests had no effect, will not understand such agonising. After all, war is either good or bad, right or wrong, yes?

No.

So on the night of the first vote, in February 2003, I supported the government, then went home with a very heavy heart, fretting in case I had made the wrong decision. A few weeks later, I had made up my mind and was probably two-to-one (in my head) in favour of invasion. It was then that I decided the time for equivocation had ended. If you're going to make a decision, stick to it, defend it and live with the consequences.

There's been a general election since then. Despite receiving more letters of criticism from constituents than on any other subject before or since, I was returned to the Commons, albeit with a reduced majority. My party suffered a greater loss of support than most people expected, losing about fifty seats. Undoubtedly Iraq was responsible for the ending of the political careers of many good people.

There have also been elections in Iraq since then. There's another one due this weekend. So was it worth it?

Those who opposed the war will never accept that. And although smaller in number, those who single mindedly, without a shadow of a doubt, called for invasion, will maintain their view as well.

I remain optimistic. I still believe that, on balance, Iraq's future holds more promise, for its people and for the wider region, than pre-invasion.

And Tony Blair remains, for me, a brilliant and principled leader who I was proud to follow into the voting lobby.

Afghanistan is about the fight against fascism

Published: July 8, 2009

John Maples, the Tory MP, asked Harriet Harman today at PMQs to remind the House why British troops were in Afghanistan. It was an appropriate question, given that the names of seven servicemen had been added to the list of the fallen at the start of the session.

The controversy that will always surround the subject of Iraq is often extended to Afghanistan. You often hear anti-war types condemning British involvement in 'Iraq and Afghanistan', as if the circumstances of our involvement were identical.

(Remember Paul Marsden? He was the Labour MP for Shrewsbury and Atcham who defected to the Lib Dems shortly after troop deployment in Afghanistan. He did so because of his opposition to the war in Afghanistan. Problem was, the Lib Dems had supported the military intervention there as well. Poor Paul...)

There is no question over the legality of action in Afghanistan, or its legitimacy in terms of UN authorisation. Given the offensive action taken against America by a certain honoured guest of the Taliban at the time, the US had no choice but to demand bin Laden be handed over. The Taliban's refusal to do so was in effect an invitation to the international community to invade. Which the international community rightly accepted.

So the legal basis for invasion and occupation was firmly established, as was the UN's moral justification. But beyond the immediate necessity of bringing bin Laden to justice, there was an added reason to support the Afghan campaign: the fight against fascism.

If you persecute gays, treat women as second-class citizens, rule by intimidation and violence, deny citizens the basic tenets of democracy and consider those of a different ethnicity, race or religion to be worthy of death and imprisonment, then you are a fascist. And the Taliban, being able to tick all of these boxes, were and remain fascists.

Some on the Left in Britain try to give the impression that they're opposed to fascism while marching in support of the Taliban and Saddam's former regime, a regime modelled deliberately on Nazism in many respects. They are liars and hypocrites. Their voices have not been listened to in this debate, and neither should they be. British soldiers are fighting and dying in the campaign to build a democratic and free Afghanistan. We should be hoping and praying for their safety and for their success against the remnants of a vile and disgusting fascist regime.

The hummus stratagem
Published: September 8, 2009

Whenever the subject of Islamist terrorism is raised, there's always someone at the back who tentatively sticks his hand up and suggests that we should negotiate with al-Qaeda in the same way we negotiated with the IRA.

Yes, well…

The thing is, although their methods were murderous and completely unacceptable, the IRA's political demands were not: civil rights for the Roman Catholic minority of Northern Ireland and unification of Ireland. Those were issues that negotiations could include. Compromises could be made. Deals could be struck.

But Islamism? Yeah, I'd like to see how that would work…

David Miliband (for it is he): Welcome to the negotiating table, Mr bin Laden. I trust you had a pleasant journey?

OBL: Indeed, yes, Foreign Secretary. CIA flights are most efficient, though uncomfortable.

DM: More comfortable than your cave, though?

OBL: Well, you'd be surprised. Mrs bin Laden and I just got a new conservatory. There's not much of a view but it's very cosy. Ooh, and we've got Sky-Plus at last! Amazing!

DM: You watch a lot of Al-Jazeera, I assume?

OBL: Well, mostly 'Dave' actually. The wife loves *Mock the Week*.

DM: Well, we have quite a lot of ground to cover. Would you like any refreshments before we start?

OBL: A little fruit, perhaps?

DM: How about this banana? I've been carrying it around for a while. No one else seems to want it... Anyway, down to business. What is your starting position in these negotiations?

OBL: Ah, yes, I have taken the liberty of writing them down (*takes paper from his wallet*). First of all, just to clear the decks, you understand, we'd like the complete destruction of the state of Israel.

DM: I see.

OBL: It's not just me, you understand, it's my organisation. They're rather old fashioned about this sort of thing. But they're sweethearts deep down, really.

DM: Yes, well, that may cause us a bit of a problem, I'm afraid. You know what the Foreign Office is like – quite conservative...

OBL: With a small 'c', I hope, eh, David!

(*Both men laugh*)

OBL: You don't mind if I call you David, do you?

DM: Of course not, Osama, of course not. The thing is, the destruction of Israel ... well, it's quite a tall order, isn't it?

OBL: Really? Oh, how disappointing. I opened with that because it was one of the more moderate of our policies.

DM: Well, not to worry. Tell you what – let's put a pin in it, as our American chums might say, and we'll put it up there and come back to it later. Sound fair?

OBL: Of course, David.

DM: So, what next?

OBL: Well, to be honest, I'm not sure how much progress we can make on this next one, given how little we made on the first...

DM: Try me.

OBL: Well, we'd like to see every American killed.

DM: I see. *Every* American citizen?

OBL: Well, perhaps that could be a matter for negotiations down the line, as you say. Perhaps initially, just those who don't like *Scrubs*. But ultimately, yes, all of the evil, Satan-worshipping dogs. What do you think? Could that be a goer, do you think?

DM: Well again, Mr bin Laden...

OBL: Osama, please.

DM: Of course, Osama... But again, that does present the government – and not just my government, but probably quite a few others – with some major diplomatic problems.

OBL: You know, David, I wouldn't want to leave here empty-handed. It would look very bad publicly.

DM: I understand the pressure you're under. You wouldn't want to lose face among your fellow Islamists.

OBL: Well, not just that. Frankie Boyle and Hugh Dennis might make fun of me again and then the wife has a field day – her and her Scottish accent! I hate it.

DM: (*Under his breath*) Yeah, I'm with you there.

Anyway, I think that's another one we might have to put a pin in and come back to later, yes? What's the third demand?

OBL: Well, it hardly seems worth it now...

DM: Don't be discouraged, Osama. Come on, try me. You never know, it might be one we can concede.

OBL: Oh, alright. Well, would it be okay to have a one-world Islamic government based on Sharia law?

DM: A one-world... I'm sorry, a what?

OBL: A one-world Islamic government based on Sharia law.

DM: And how would that work, exactly?

OBL: Oh, it basically does what it says on the tin: one world, so, you know, everyone's included, and inclusiveness always goes down well in the West, yeah? Islamic, obviously. And based on Sharia Law which, in its favour – and I can see that look of scepticism in your face, David, but bear with me – which in its favour is given by

God and therefore is perfect, unlike man-made laws. So, you know … everyone wins.

DM: Everyone?

OBL: Well, not women, obviously. Frankly, I don't see a place in the government for Harriet Harman.

DM: And is there a downside?

OBL: Everyone else would have to convert to my particular form of Islam, obviously. And no gays allowed. To be honest, I don't anticipate a particularly warm welcome for the Worldwide Caliphate from the LGBTs.

DM: Osama, I wonder if we could…

OBL: Put a pin in it?

DM: Yes, would you mind?

OBL: Well, if you insist, but I'm not sure where we could go from here.

DM: I was hoping we could agree something on a slightly more modest scale.

OBN: For instance?

DM: Well, how about hummus?

OBL: Hummus?

DM: Some bright spark in the FCO thought of it, and I think it's splendid. We ditch any idea of destroying Israel, killing Americans or abolishing all non-Sharia governments in the world, and instead we offer free hummus to you, your organisation and all their dependents.

OBL: Hmmm... Okay, it's a deal!

It's personal

Class warfare

Published: June 7, 2008

An amusing (I think) anecdote which illuminates class differences in Scotland perfectly, and therefore can only be understood if you imagine the exchange detailed below taking place with Scottish accents.

My wife, Carolyn, while in her very first job after leaving school, was approached by a co-worker who asked, in a broad Glasgow accent: 'So, do you live in a boat hoose?'

'Pardon?'

'Do you live in a boat hoose?'

Carolyn, completely bewildered, replied: 'You mean, a canal barge?'

'Naw! A BOAT HOOSE! Do you live in a boat hoose or a cooncil hoose?'

Selfish nation

Published: January 27, 2009

Have you ever tried to use the 'parent and toddler' parking spaces at a supermarket and found all the bays being used by people who are obviously *sans enfants*?

Silly question. If you're the parent of small children and you own a car and you shop at a supermarket, then I know this has happened to you. Just as I know that you've seen plenty of dog owners allowing their pets to crap on the pavement and not clean up after them. Parents double-parking outside schools, obscuring the view of pupils crossing the road? Playing loud music at night with no consideration for your neighbours?

What else? Let's see... I'm sure readers can come up with their own infuriating examples of how selfish and thoughtless our society seems to have become. It's not even that those who are guilty of such misdemeanours are necessarily bad people. What's more worrying is that small acts of selfishness seem to be more tolerated today then they were in the past and perpetrated by more people than ever before.

Take parking. There are streets in my constituency which were built without the foresight to predict the massive increase in car ownership, and so today are physically incapable of providing enough on-road car parking. So residents, perfectly understandably and unavoidably, have to park at least two wheels on the pavement.

But there are many, many other roads which are wide enough to allow for on-road parking on both sides while allowing a safe flow-through of traffic. So no need to park on the pavement, right? Wrong. Never mind if parents with pushchairs or people in wheelchairs can no longer get past without having to use the road, no, no, no. What matters is that your car doesn't get scratched by passing traffic.

Rat-runs through residential areas? Making roads less safe for children is surely a small price to pay if you can avoid a set of traffic lights and take, oh, seconds, at least, off the length of your journey.

In my home town of Beith, a new children's fenced-off play area has been constructed by the local council. It has a strict 'no dogs' policy, but that didn't stop one woman taking her dog in there for some exercise. When my sister accosted her, the woman's defence was: 'But this is the only place where I know my dog can't wander off!'

A debate is raging, mostly on the right wing of UK politics, about the alleged pettiness of some of the new laws and offences that have been introduced by the government (although to read some of the complaints. you'd think littering wasn't an offence before 1997).

I actually do understand the reservations about the plethora of anti-social legislation introduced in the last twelve years. The difference between the government's critics and me is that they think it has all been unnecessary, whereas I *wish* it was unnecessary.

Without legal enforcement and the consequent media coverage, how can we expect people to improve their behaviour, to consider others before they behave selfishly?

And I ask in a genuine spirit of enquiry. Is there another way to remind us of our obligations to each other and not just to ourselves? I have no wish to criminalise millions of law-abiding citizens, but neither do I want to tolerate millions of people's quality of life being compromised by the thoughtless behaviour of others.

Twenty-five random things about me
Published: February 3, 2009

Iain Dale was a big fan of 'blog memes', which challenged various bloggers to write whimsical posts on the same theme. This was written in response to such a challenge.

So, twenty-five random things... Let's see...

1. I missed two months of primary school because of whooping cough and my teacher gave me extra lessons to catch up when I returned.
2. In 1982 I applied to join the police.
3. In 1982 I was rejected by the police because I had acne. True story.
4. I once slept on the pavement outside the Apollo in Glasgow queuing for Genesis tickets.
5. I once opened the door of a moving train in a pathetic attempt to impress a girl.
6. I've seen *Shock Treatment*, the sequel to *The Rocky Horror Picture Show*, sixteen times.
7. The first time I drove a fork-lift truck, I crashed it.
8. I wooed Carolyn by juggling oranges.
9. I own all seven seasons of 'Buffy' on DVD.
10. I have driven a fork-lift truck on only one occasion.

11. I was once caught nicking a roll of Sellotape from a newsagent.

12. In 1990, I visited a brothel. In a purely professional capacity, of course.

13. I've seen Buck's Fizz play live. Twice.

14. I scored precisely zero in an electronics exam when I was studying mechanical engineering.

15. I played Lieutenant Bogust in my school's 1981 stage version of *Whisky Galore*!

16. In the '70s, I founded a Steve (*Six Million Dollar Man*) Austin fan club. It was not a successful venture.

17. I once threw a banger (firework, not sausage) at an off-duty policeman.

18. I got lost in Paris during a school trip.

19. I once gave my big brother's new two-piece suit to the rag-and-bone man in return for a yellow balloon.

20. I was, briefly, a member of a Christian drama group called 'Ripples'.

21. I first sang karaoke on holiday with Carolyn in Salou in 1997.

22. The first time I was ever in a plane was to do a parachute jump.

23. My all-time favourite book is *The Taste of Too Much* by Cliff Hanley.

24. My favourite album is *Selling England By The Pound* by Genesis.

25. I often worry that blogging is taking over my life.

The People vs George Lucas

Published: February 14, 2009

Everyone remembers the day they first saw *Star Wars*, right?

Of course they do. For me, it was Thursday 2 February 1978. That was also the day that issue #1 of *Star Wars Weekly* went on sale and I grasped my copy in my hands as I waited anxiously for my dad, exhausted after a typically hard day driving his HGV, to respond to my desperate plea to drive me, my sister and my best friend, Brem, all the way to Glasgow, the only place within travelling distance where the movie phenomenon was showing.

He reluctantly relented, and the five of us – including mum – piled into our tiny yellow Nissan and headed for the big city, Brem and I barely able to contain our excitement. The local cinema in Beith, the George, was a regular and familiar experience by then, but neither of us had seen the inside of the legendary Odeon in Glasgow's Renfield Street.

Dad quickly found a parking space. History does not record if it was legal or safe, but I don't recall him getting a parking ticket that night. We walked the short journey to the Odeon, and were appalled to see the queue! None of us had ever seen a queue that long for anything! No way were we going to get a seat inside. But we joined it anyway. Even that bit was fun; the air of excitement was palpable, and not just among the younger members of the crowd. Buskers and beggars took advantage of their captive audience to entertain and embarrass (my dad dryly informed us that one old soul was getting no money from him because he 'never gave me a song'...).

And, faster than any of us expected, we were moving towards the Odeon entrance. Would we get in, or would we be stopped just short of the prize, a 'Sorry – full up' sign barring our way between us and that far, far away galaxy?

We got in. And so did a couple of hundred people behind us. A big place, the Odeon, it turned out.

The atmosphere inside was electric. And even the advertisers joined in the spirit of the occasion, having produced sci-fi-themed commercials specially to be shown before the main feature. At one point, a breathless hush descended when words resembling 'A long time ago, in a galaxy far, far away...' appeared on screen, to be followed by ... the Mash men (oh, come on! You must remember them: they sounded like Daleks and every advert ended with the words 'then they smash them all to bits', with the wee metal aliens collapsing in fits of giggles). And then there was the ad where a golden robot being constructed in a production line has his head fastened on back-to-front, and consoles himself with a Hamlet cigar to the sound of 'Air on a G String'.

And then, at last, after weeks and months of hype, of listening to the disco version of the *Star Wars* theme by Meco, of reading every morsel of information about the movie and its stars in every magazine and newspaper (Alec Guinness, we discovered, had been in a number of films before *Star Wars*), the 20th Century Fox logo appeared on screen, accompanied by that famous fanfare. Followed closely by *that* fanfare…

Both Brem and I, and a number of our friends had already read the novelisation of *Star Wars*. More than once. Nothing in the plot of the movie we were about to see was going to surprise us. We knew every twist, every conflict, every argument, every fight and every resolution. We already knew most of the dialogue and we were able, that night, immediately to identify, to our horror, which scenes included in the novel were *not* part of the finished film. That was the first time we realised that there can sometimes be differences in the content of novels and the movies on which they're based.

Such triflings aside, it's fair to say that that night in February more than thirty years ago, I fell in love with *Star Wars*. You had me at 'long ago', as it were.

Even Dad fell for it. On the way back home along the M8, our Nissan Sunny became an X-Wing rebel fighter, darting in and out of lanes as Dad shot down the enemy TIE fighters in front of us.

So I was hooked, as were millions of kids my age – and many of different ages – throughout the planet. *Star Wars* helped define our childhoods. No one had ever seen anything like it. It helped rejuvenate not only the science fiction genre, but Hollywood itself, as well as making cinema-going fashionable again after some very fallow years and spawning loads of very questionable rip-offs and 'homages'.

Even then, back in 1978, my friends and I were aware of some of Luke Skywalker's and Obi-Wan Kenobi's back-stories; that Luke's father, a Jedi Knight, had been betrayed and murdered by

Darth Vader who was in turn almost killed by Kenobi, who threw Vader into a volcanic pit. He had been rescued by Imperial storm troopers who had only managed to save his life by placing him in a black life-support suit.

The movie sequels were, inevitably, keenly anticipated by us and by the rest of the world. *Empire* was magnificent, *Return* disappointing. And I still believe it was a fundamental mistake by George Lucas to make Luke and Leia brother and sister. Big mistake.

Fast forward sixteen years to the release of *Star Wars Episode I: The Phantom Menace*. I tried to like it, I really did. I even saw it in the cinema three times before buying it on VHS and then DVD. It took me another few years and two further prequels for me to admit they were crap. The first sequel seemed to be primarily about tax reform. The second and third could have been magnificent. They were not.

My own theory is that Lucas was too close to his baby to be trusted with directing all three prequels. It's significant that the best film of the whole series, *The Empire Strikes Back*, was directed by Irvin Kershner, not Lucas. Had Lucas given the basic story of Episodes I to III to another writer and director, they would, I'm sure, have produced far superior movies. Those films made perfect sense to the man who wrote them and who has lived with their development most of his life, but for the rest of us, the reaction was 'Huh?'

As Simon Pegg screamed at the crying child holding the Jar-Jar Binks figurine in *Spaced*: 'You don't understand, you weren't there!'

And that's even before I get on to the re-issues of the original three movies in 1997 to mark the series' twentieth birthday. On that subject, I will say only this: Han Solo shot Greedo first and quite right.

Which brings me, not very neatly, to what inspired this rather lengthy post, and I should offer a hat-tip to Tom Watson for this. *The People vs George Lucas*, from what I can gather, is a movie that explores some of the issues I've raised in this post and which have been regularly discussed by *Star Wars* fans for decades. It's due for release next year and, while I accept it's aimed at a fairly narrow audience, I have a feeling I may well be queuing at a cinema once more.

Striking out

Published: March 7, 2009

I've always maintained that it was the miners' strike in 1984/85 that politicised me and brought me into the Labour Party. But that's only partly true.

Because if I'm honest, the miners' strike probably delayed my joining. I was already keen to become a member, but was uneasy about the reasons for Scargill calling a strike and appalled by his refusal to put his decision to a national ballot of the NUM membership. And I was disappointed that the Labour leadership seemed to be silent, or at least ambivalent, on the matter. Eventually I decided to join *despite* my reservations about the party's relationship with the NUM; I figured I could do more good inside the tent (metaphors involving urination and camping equipment were unfamiliar to me at the time).

I found it easy, however, to distinguish between support for the NUM leadership and support for the miners and their families. I had no problem with the latter and donated as much as I could to various appeals for support. Even the friends I had grown up with in Beith felt politicised enough to make Nazi salutes at the Yuill & Dodds lorries which were helping to break the strike by transporting coke between Hunterston in Ayrshire and Ravenscraig steelworks in Motherwell, using the Beith by-pass as part of their route. Even this childish gesture (which actually succeeded in annoying the drivers, from what we could tell from their responses) provoked doubts in my mind later on when I considered what the impact would have been on the workers of Ravenscraig if the supplies actually stopped.

And despite my objections to Scargill privately, I quickly found myself defending 'the line' when arguing with college friends who couldn't understand the absence of a ballot.

On the Sunday in March 1985, when TV programmes were interrupted to bring the nation the news that the NUM executive had finally conceded the inevitable and announced a return to work, I cried.

In his biography of Neil Kinnock, published during the 1987 general election campaign, Michael Leapman describes the strike as Kinnock's 'wasted year'. It was a year when the Labour leader was able to make virtually no progress in driving his party's electoral recovery because the only narratives the media were interested in were Scargill vs Kinnock, Scargill vs Thatcher and the NUM's relationship with Labour. And the running sore throughout it all was Scargill's Stalinist arrogance in refusing his members the right to say whether or not they disagreed with him.

Eric Hammond, leader of the electricians' union, subsequently risked the wrath of Labour conference delegates by describing the miners as 'lions led by donkeys', a reference I found particularly apt at the time.

The *Sunday Times* once described Scargill as 'the man who fought the class war, and lost it'. He also played a key role in helping Thatcher define herself as a Prime Minister willing to face down the unions. She has every reason to be grateful to Scargill for the immense political favour he did her and her party.

And the ultimate irony, of course, is that a quarter of a century later, we've realised the mistake we made in allowing the mines to be closed.

As a new party member at the time, the miners' strike presented me with a range of difficult political questions, some of which I dodged and others I confronted head-on. It wasn't an ideal time to join the Labour Party, nor a comfortable time to be a member.

For me, it was a political baptism of fire. For thousands of miners and their families, it was rather more serious. Some lost their homes, many more found themselves in financial dire straits, families were split down the middle, marriages collapsed under the pressure, children went hungry, strikers went to jail, lost their jobs.

And even by the 1992 general election, Labour hadn't recovered politically from the damage inflicted on it by Scargill's arrogance.

For all the folk songs and rose-tinted retrospectives in the last few days, I have a feeling that Conservatives probably look back on the strike with more positive feelings than do Labour supporters.

A quarter of a century and counting
Published: April 18, 2009

Twenty-five years ago this week, I finally decided to join the Labour Party.

The decision was made after a lot of introspection. I knew I wanted to get involved in politics; in the early 1980s it was difficult not to be affected by political events all around us: the inner city riots of 1981, the Falklands War, the splits in the Labour Party and Benn's challenge for Labour's deputy leadership, mass unemployment (particularly in north Ayrshire, where I grew up), Thatcher's 1983 landslide and the year-long miners' strike.

Both my parents had voted Labour throughout their lives, as had their parents. My maternal grandfather had been a great fan of Tony Benn in the 1960s (and was therefore a natural recruit for the SDP when it was formed in 1981). And, on the occasion of my first vote – the 1982 regional council elections – I dutifully turned up at the polling station to support the Labour candidate, Jimmy Jennings.

But a year later, the first time I had the chance to vote in a general election, I just couldn't bring myself to vote for a party led by Michael Foot, even though I was living in a marginal seat at the time. Along with two friends who were also voting in a general election for the first time, I put my cross against the SDP candidate's name (as described in a post I wrote last year). As happened in numerous seats across the country, the third party managed to split the Labour vote, allowing the Tory candidate to win.

Fast forward another year, and despite my brief and accidental membership of the Conservative Party, I knew that that was the one party I just couldn't consider joining (actually, there were two parties I wouldn't have considered joining, but the SNP didn't even qualify as a candidate to be rejected). Neil Kinnock's election as Labour's leader had grabbed my attention: here was somebody who was serious about opposing the Tories and, at last, serious about turning Labour into a government-in-waiting, rather than an umbrella pressure group pandering to every minority interest under the sun. I still had my reservations about policy: I didn't support unilateral nuclear disarmament and thought Labour's previous policy of disengagement with Europe was bonkers. But they would be ditched in time, I figured. So when, at the end of a party political broadcast, an address was given for membership enquiries, I bit the bullet and sent off a letter.

Funny how a seemingly casual decision at the time could have such a massive effect on the course of someone's life. But the truth is I never considered it to be a casual decision. I took it extremely seriously at the time and, in the years that followed, my commitment to the Labour tribe defined my career and even my personal relationships. Personal and political highlights became indistinguishable: when Kinnock made his anti-Militant speech to Labour conference in Bournemouth in 1985, I was house-sitting for a friend in Sale, whooping and air-punching in a room occupied by a total of one person. On a related note, 1988 will always resonate in my memory as the year I was served with an interim interdict (injunction) due to my involvement in a local constituency inquiry into the activities of Militant members in Cathcart.

The low points have regularly outnumbered the high points: defeat in the 1987 and 1992 general elections (the consequences of the latter being the loss of my job when I had just bought a house and started a family), the loss of the Scottish* by-election in 1988, John Smith's death in 1994, my rejection as a Labour candidate for the local elections in 1990, the attempted coup against Tony Blair in 2006.

But the highlights made everything seem worth it: the morning of 2 May 1997, my selection as Cathcart's parliamentary candidate in September 2000 and subsequent election as an MP in June 2001, my appointment as Scottish Labour's press officer in September 1990, my first speech to national conference in September 1989, my appointment as a minister in September 2006 (September seems to be an important month for me, I've just realised).

Something of a roller coaster ride, you might conclude. As I've often told Carolyn: I've never understood those who claim politics is dull. It's more entertaining than the best soap opera, with more interesting and better-written characters.

And in the last quarter of a century, I've never regretted for an instant my decision to pick up a pen and notepad as that party political broadcast came to an end and jot down the address, '150 Walworth Road, London'.

* *In the same way actors refer to* Macbeth *as 'the Scottish play', that's how I tend to refer to Jim Sillars' former seat.*

The 'firsts' meme
Published: April 27, 2009

Yet another meme from the odd mind of Iain Dale.

First Job
Dressing up as a giant seagull (whose name was Irwin C. Gull - geddit?) during the Merrymas Parade in Irvine, Ayrshire. As Gene Kelly said in *Singin' In The Rain*: 'Dignity, always dignity...'

First Real Job
Staff writer with *Business Scotland* magazine, 1986.

First Role in Politics
Constituency delegate to Scottish Labour conference in Perth. 1988.

First Car
B-reg Ford Fiesta, bought second hand in 1988. Got well ripped off.

First Record
'Northern Lights' by Renaissance was the first single I bought myself, and it remains one of my all-time favourite songs. But the first single I actually owned was 'Happiness' by Ken Dodd.

First Football Match
St Mirren vs Bristol City in the quarter final (second leg) of the Anglo Scottish Cup, Love Street, 26 September, 1978.

First Concert
John Martyn at the Glasgow Pavilion, 1982.

First Country Visited
France, school trip in 1979.

First TV Appearance
Speech to Labour conference, Brighton, 1989.

First Political Speech
Scottish Labour conference, Perth, 1988. Can't really remember the details.

First Girlfriend/Boyfriend
Lesley Bell. She was in the same chemistry class at Garnock Academy.

First Encounter with a Famous Person
When I interviewed Shirley Williams when she visited East Kilbride in 1986. I was a cub reporter.

First Brush With Death
In 1983, I opened the door of a slam-door train carriage while it was travelling between Glasgow and Paisley. It was an accident, honest! I tried to close it by leaning out, but we were still travelling too fast for me to be able to pull it shut. As I sat back down, defeated, another train, traveling in the opposite direct, passed us. I think I may have had a narrow escape.

First House/Flat Owned
Second floor flat at 493 Clarkston Road, Muirend, Glasgow. No blue plaque up yet, I can't help noticing.

First Film Seen at a Cinema
Oliver! at a cinema in Saltcoats.

First Time on the Radio
Radio Clyde, 1994. I had to answer questions about roadworks being carried out by my employer, Strathclyde Regional Council, the following weekend.

First Politician I Met
My local MP, David Lambie, during one of the 1974 elections. My pals and I asked him for his autograph!

First Book I Remember Reading
The Wolves of Willoughby Chase by Joan Aiken.

First Visit to the London Palladium
Never been. Does the Glasgow Apollo count? (In which case, to see Rick Wakeman in 1982).

First Election
1986 Regional Council Elections in Edinburgh. Labour won back control of Lothian Regional Council. I spent the evening as a 'runner' for BBC Radio Scotland, carrying results notes to their reporter at Meadowbank Stadium.

A twit woos
Published: February 14, 2010

'Get your coat, love, you've pulled.' Or how about 'I hope you know CPR because you've just taken my breath away'?

Or even the one immortalised in the Bellamy Brothers' classic 1979 hit, 'If I said you had a beautiful body would you hold it against me?'

Have any of those lines ever actually worked? Surely not.

The reason I ask is that Carolyn and I were chatting the other night about how we first got together. Sometimes we look at Ronnie and Reggie and wonder how on earth it actually happened. And what better day than today to reminisce...?

We were working in the same department of a large local authority. (Pointless detail: our boss was John Brown, big brother of Gordon. Scotland's a very small place.) She was based in the office on the floor below the press office, where I worked. Occasionally she would be despatched upstairs to help out in the press office. And I ... well, I *noticed* her. I mean, *everybody* notices Carolyn. But the thing I noticed the most was that she was completely out of my league.

Did that stop me? Put it this way: if someone has the self-confidence, even arrogance, to believe he would one day make a good MP, would being regarded by a girl as something she'd just stepped in dissuade him?

Because here's the basic truth about me and Carolyn: she doesn't like me very much. Never has, never will. Oh, she loves me, I've no doubt about that. But we always roll our eyes whenever someone on TV says something like 'I married my best friend.' I mean, if I'd married my best friend I'd be living in Brighton right now with a gay, male psychiatric nurse who at least shares my enthusiasm for sci-fi.

So, no, Carolyn and I would never describe ourselves as 'friends', best or otherwise.

Anyway, back to 1996...

She didn't like me and she made that clear to me whenever she saw me. I had a cat and a dog at the same time when I was a boy, and the dog loved the cat. It was always trying to be its friend, trying to get the cat to play with it. The cat wasn't interested, would ignore the dog's overtures or, occasionally, swat it away with a dismissive flick of her fully-extended claws. Well, you get the picture...

But perseverance is a wonderful thing. As Carolyn admits today, I wore her down.

I had a three-pronged strategy. The first was juggling (obviously). I'd use any excuse to walk downstairs to her office on some pretext or other. And when I did, I just happened to be carrying three oranges with me. And then I would nonchalantly juggle them within sight of her desk. In my mind she was re-assessing her view of the big guy from upstairs. In reality, she just tutted more loudly.

But she must have warmed towards me, because soon I was showing her my holiday photos, CDs I'd just bought, my scars...

Then there was her major Achilles' Heel: public transport. Or rather, her aversion to it. She didn't have a car at the time and I did. So I quickly realised that offering her a lift home would win many brownie points. That was how we actually got to spend more and more time together, just the two of us. And even when the traffic was heavy and the journey home seemed to be lasting longer and longer each day, she didn't seem to mind.

She was also impressed at my knowledge of astronomy, though in truth, I'd become a bit rusty since I'd hoovered up Patrick Moore's *Observer's Guide* as a teenager. So as I walked her to her mum's front door, I would authoritatively point out the lesser-known constellations to her, such as 'the Great Barbecue', the 'Teakettle' and 'Merlin's Armpit'...

Ah, how time passes when you're in love. One minute I was dropping her off at her mum's, the next it seems we were returning from our honeymoon.

Everyone's relationship is unique and special. How couples actually get together is a real-life drama (or sometimes sitcom) in which most of us play a role at some point.

This, I thought, would be a good idea for a blog meme, but I'm not going to nominate anyone else to volunteer their own experiences of how they met and wooed their partners. Those are personal details that not everyone will be keen to share. But if anyone – other bloggers or readers of this one – care to offer some juicy or funny details, then please do.

And if anyone has ever successfully used the line 'Did the sun come out or did you just smile at me?', I need to know.

Highs and lows
Published: March 23, 2010

Now would be as good a time as any to reflect on the parliament just about to end and consider some of the best and worst bits, speaking from a personal point of view. It's funny how I've started to compartmentalise my life into four- or five-year parliaments...

First, the 'lows'.

And there are a lot to choose from, aren't there? My sacking as a minister in October 2008 is certainly up there as one of the worst points of my political life. Then there was the coup by fellow backbenchers in September 2006, which led to Tony Blair announcing he would resign as PM earlier than he had promised. But since I want to maintain my friendship with some of those involved, I will write no more about that. For now.

I had intended to include the hysterical over-reaction by the media to my 'Heaven knows we're miserable now' post as one of my lows, but in hindsight, I think I managed the fallout quite well and even enjoyed it, so I won't. I would, however, list being told to pull out of *Question Time* as a consequence of that furore as one of the definite lows of the last five years.

And there was, of course, the expenses scandal, the reporting of which by *The Telegraph* made Westminster a hellish place to be for the second half of last year. But for me, the lowest low point came only indirectly from that. When I was first elected to Parliament in June 2001, my mum and dad came to the count to see me declared winner in Glasgow Cathcart, as the seat was then known. Mum was excited and overjoyed when, before the formal announcement, I told her what my majority was. I have never seen Dad, who has never been particularly expressive, look more proud. Having a son become an MP was quite a thing for a working-class family from Ayrshire.

Eight years on, Dad told me recently of a conversation he had struck up with a stranger during a train journey to see my older brother in Stockport. The man asked Dad what his sons did for a living. Dad said to me later: 'I didn't want to admit that you were an MP...'

I was utterly shocked, although I didn't let that show. The thing is, I didn't blame him. And for a while last year, as a result of what he said and because of the general fall-out from the expenses scandal, I seriously considered not standing again. After all, who wants to be in a job where your family are ashamed of you? Other things happened to change my mind and slowly I emerged from my despondency. But that revelation was uncontestably the lowest point of the 2005 parliament for me.

Fortunately, there have been plenty of 'highs' to provide a balance.

A happier consequence of that September 2006 coup mentioned above was my own elevation to ministerial office at the Department for Transport. There then followed a two-year long high for me. Yes, there were drawbacks, less time with the family being the main one, and on two occasions – one political and one personal – I drafted resignation letters which I intended to send but never did. But it was an experience I wouldn't have missed for anything, and I will always be grateful to Tony and then Gordon (who reappointed me in June 2007) for the opportunity.

Another high point has been this blog. Go figure.

But for me, the highest of all the high points has been a purely personal one. In June 2006, Carolyn gave birth to our second son, referred to on this site as Reggie (not his real name, in case you ask, and neither is Ronnie his big brother's real name). Nothing puts the fluff and nonsense of politics into perspective better than the arrival of a wee, fat (9lbs, 2oz believe it or not!) gurgling, baldy baby.

His arrival also gave me an opportunity to do something that every man should do at least once: drive through a dozen sets of red lights at six in the morning while your wife tries to avoid going into labour on the passenger seat.

So there we have it. If I'm lucky enough to be returned to serve in the next parliament, there will undoubtedly be highs and lows to write about in another four or five years' time. A few more of the 'highs' and few less 'lows' would be nice. But politics is never like that, is it?

New media

Busy doing lunch

Published: May 14, 2008

Sorry for not posting earlier, but what with PMQs, the post-match analysis with Iain Dale and then lunch with same, it's been crazy! Iain was very good company and had tons of very interesting and funny anecdotes, none of which I can use here, sadly (just as he can't use any of mine – you hear that, Dale?).

Then an odd thing happened. I was half way through my chicken Caesar salad when suddenly the lights started to flicker, dark clouds obscured the sun, a wind started howling through the restaurant, a black crow squawked and flew into the air and a young baby started crying. For none other than Paul Staines (aka Guido Fawkes) had entered the restaurant. 'Don't look into his eyes!' I whispered urgently to Iain as he rose to say hello. But it was too late...

The olives and balsamic vinegar were nice, though.

It's nice to be wanted (or so I'm told)

Published: December 19, 2008

The car crash that was the launch of LabourList and Derek Draper's involvement therein became the talk of the blogosphere for a while. Fortunately, with Derek's departure, LabourList has become a first-class read and a serious forum for the party.

Those who suspected that this blog was nothing more than a Labour put-up job, aimed purely at broadcasting the party line, can rest easy.

Because if this were simply a Labour HQ mouthpiece, surely I would have been invited to Derek Draper's Labour blogathon taking place tomorrow?

Alas, I only found out about this prestigious event by reading Iain Dale's Diary. I discovered the names of those invited to participate by reading Guido. And I found out I was not the only snubbed Labour blogger by reading Chris Paul.

I texted a friend who *is* on the invitation list, and he texted back to apologise and to say that, although it wasn't his gig, he would make sure I was invited to future events. I responded in an unseasonably huffy manner: 'Don't bother.'

After all, there is surely some value in not being seen as part of an official Labour-oriented blogging circle, and I don't think I would take kindly to being 'expected' to blog certain subjects if I wasn't already planning to do so anyway.

Nevertheless, I feel the snub personally. Maybe, after the fake memo, the 'Heaven knows we're miserable now' fiasco and my *X-Factor* live thread, I'm not considered a 'serious' blogger? Ah, who cares – I've got my latest Christmas hit to post, plus my favourite all-time James Bond movies to schedule for publication on Christmas Day.

But I'll bet they'll regret not having me there when they get to item four on tomorrow's agenda: '*Doctor Who*, season four – parallels for Labour's fourth term'.

So, Christmas quiz time: what's the most likely reason for a line being put through my name when the list of invitees was being drawn up? Keep it clean, people…

Your chance to shine
Published: January 5, 2009

This was written in sheer frustration at the demented nature of many of the comments I received to the most innocuous and non-political posts. What is it about people who comment on political blogs?

I've decided to introduce another award – this time for the most irrelevant and ridiculously partisan political response to a non-political post.

A brilliant example – and the first winner – is this response to my post on Saturday welcoming the casting of Matt Smith in the lead role in *Doctor Who*:

'And, of course, he's a Labour supporter too. Bound to be a great success, don't you think?'

Fantastic! Now, that's what blogging's about.

I can't wait to see other entertaining examples this year of commenters having a pop at the BBC/public sector workers/ Europe/Gordon Brown/me on the back of posts about *Doctor Who* or *The X-Factor*.

But please, no hoaxes: the competition is open only to genuinely confused and bewildered readers.

For whom the wife Twitters
Published: February 26, 2009

The Hansard Society's panel on MPs and new media on Tuesday evening was videoed by Microsoft (the hosts of the seminar and the sponsors of the report, *MPs online*) and will be available online shortly, so I hope I can't be accused of telling tales out of school...

The speakers were me, Douglas Carswell, Lynne Featherstone and Lib Dem MEP Graham Watson. It was a good discussion and some of the points I made about the need to respect bloggers' and commenters' preference for anonymity will no doubt be debated further when the video goes online.

But it was comments by Graham Watson which will, I fear, come back to haunt him. He first of all admitted that his staff had trawled Facebook in order to generate 'friends' for him – something I find quite ridiculous; is that really what Facebook is for, building a network of people you've never heard of so that you can win a 'mine's bigger than yours' competition?

Secondly, and more bizarrely, he boasted that he doesn't update his own Twitter. 'But the person who does it on my behalf knows me very well – my wife!'

If you're going to 'do' new media, you should do it honestly. Every person who follows Graham Watson on Twitter will now know that they're not actually following him, but his wife pretending to be him.

Does this matter? Not to Graham, obviously, but yes, I think it does. If I didn't have the time to Twitter, I wouldn't do it. But it's only 140 characters, for crying out loud! How long does that take anyone?

The case for blog regulation
Published: April 1, 2009

Quite a few people fell hook, line and sinker for this one, I'm delighted to report. Even Guido Fawkes carried a companion piece over on his own blog, linking to this.

After much thought and consideration, I spoke in favour of the Regulation of New Media Bill in the Commons last night.

The essential purpose of the legislation, as Andy Burnham, the Culture, Media and Sport Secretary, told the House, is to make sure that new media, like blogs and social networking sites, can't be used by terrorists (and I accept this is where there will be some disagreement in the blogscape: 'terrorists' are defined under Schedule 1 to the Bill as 'anyone who pursues a persistent pattern of anti-social or irritating behaviour, such behaviour to be defined as double parking, parking in parent-and-toddler spaces at supermarkets, talking loudly in cinemas or any other activity as defined by the Secretary of State').

The Bill will also introduce mandatory 'politeness and decency' standards (the so-called The Clarkson Rules) which will allow any blog author to be fined if he or she allows any foul language to be used in their comments section. Andy expressed some surprise that this part of the Bill had received the private backing of none other than Paul Staines (aka Guido Fawkes).

But by far the most controversial part of the Bill is the section that demands that, from April 2010, every British blogger will have to submit each post for official approval. My main concern is with regard to the turnaround time; the whole point of blogging could be rendered meaningless or at least blunted if we're unable to respond timeously to current events. Andy, however, managed to reassure me and the House that posts will be approved by the new regulatory body, BlogOff, within about thirty-six hours.

This drew sage nods from Tory blogger Iain Dale who was in the Strangers' Gallery to watch the debate at first hand. In fact he and I had discussed the Bill earlier in the day after I happened upon him, Derek Draper, Alex Hilton and Tim Ireland having a jovial and relaxed meal together in the Terrace Canteen.

The Second Reading of the Regulation of New Media Bill was agreed without a vote and surprisingly little comment, either in the mainstream media or in the blogscape.

There will, inevitably, be those who will cry 'Big Brother!', even at such light-touch regulatory measures. But blogging can only benefit and prosper with the official stamp of approval from HMG.

I welcome your comments.

UPDATE at 1.45 pm: Admit it, I had some of you there, didn't I? Come on, admit it! You know who you are…

So, what did I miss?

Published: April 12, 2009

On the day that 'Smeargate' was first splashed across the front page of the Daily Telegraph, *I was woken by a phone call from a Labour MP and friend who was seeking to encourage me to use my blog to advance The Line. And The Line was that the real story was not that Damian McBride had conspired, along with Derek Draper, to smear not only members of the Opposition, but – unforgivably – their spouses. No, the real story was the question of how right-wing blogger Guido Fawkes got hold of McBride's private emails in the first place. I sighed deeply. 'That's not the story,' I told my disappointed friend.*

I had planned to end my self-imposed break from blogging tomorrow rather than today, but events, dear boy, events…

First, I think it's important that Labour people make clear - and are *seen* to make clear - that this whole McBride/Draper episode (must we call it 'Smeargate'? Really?) is as inexcusable to us as it is to the rest of the world. There is absolutely no point in anyone in the party trying to spin such an odious sequence of events, of trying to suggest that it's less serious than what the media are attempting to make out.

To those comrades who might feel tempted to downplay this episode, to dismiss it simply as 'two friends exchanging not-very-serious emails', I would pose a question: how would Labour have reacted if this smear had been aimed at the partners of Labour politicians and had been perpetrated by a senior civil servant in a Conservative administration? Go on, think about that before trying to dismiss this as a storm in a teacup.

And there's no point in talking up the question of how these emails found their way into Guido's possession. Do you imagine for even a moment that the electorate could possibly care less about that? It's insulting to imagine that this can be turned into a 'process' story with Derek Draper's email account, or Derek himself, portrayed as the 'victim'.

Of course, McBride had to go — that was obvious to everyone with an ounce of judgment from the second this story broke. How could Number 10 have even tried to recover from this fiasco while the perpetrator was safely ensconced? Which brings me to my next point: I can understand why the Tories might privately have hoped McBride would survive. After all, what could be more damaging to the government and to the Prime Minister himself than to be seen to endorse such behaviour by taking no action against him? The Tories were handed an enormous propaganda gift this weekend; to have protected McBride's position in Number 10 would have made it the gift that keeps on giving.

So, yes, I can understand why the Tories would have preferred McBride to remain in post. But what on earth was Draper thinking when he told various media outlets yesterday that he didn't think McBride should have had to resign?

But this isn't about positioning or spinning or misdirection or whatever. This is about standards of political activity, standards which have fallen far, far below what is remotely acceptable, especially for someone working at the very heart of government.

We screwed up, big time. We have no one – absolutely no one at all – to blame for this but ourselves. The damage the Labour Party and the government have sustained these last twenty-four hours has been entirely self-inflicted.

And the people behind this sordid little mess owe everyone named in these emails a very public apology.

The ethic of progressive blogging: good luck with that
Published: April 20, 2009

Sunder Katwala's statement published on Liberal Conspiracy is a well-meaning and thoughtful response to the sheer awfulness of what's happened in the Drapersphere in the last couple of weeks.

It's all good stuff: 'We believe we must act as ambassadors for the political values we profess... We oppose the politics of personal destruction... We do not believe that the internet is inevitably a force for anti-politics... We believe that we can challenge our political opponents without always questioning their integrity...'

My only issue with it is that it sounds just a tad defensive. However well placed McBride and Draper were, their activities never reflected on me, on this blog or on the many, many other good Labour-inclined bloggers out there. I don't feel I have anything to prove, even in the wake of what will inevitably come to be seen as the nadir of Labour's activities in the new media.

Item 4 in Sundar's statement, under the sub-heading 'Independent spaces', says:

'We believe that attempts to transfer "command and control" models to online politics will inevitably fail.'

That's the part with which I agree most. Labour bloggers should, of course, network and share ideas. But the idea that we can be organised under a single strategy imposed from party HQ is laughable and a waste of time, doomed to fail. Such an approach flies in the face of the reality of the blogscape, namely that blogging has always been, and will always be, a grassroots activity, drawing its strength and momentum from a disparate range of individuals, not from organisations or institutions.

Well, that's what I think, anyway.

And the reason I won't sign up explicitly to 'The ethic of progressive blogging' is, firstly, that it sounds a bit too much like a standard imposed on individual bloggers by the wider community.

Secondly, as I said above, I don't feel I have anything to prove; if readers want to know about my ethics and those of this blog, they should read my posts.

Signing up to this statement, valuable though it may be, won't guarantee that any site's content will conform to any such standards, just as not signing up to it won't mean my own posts will fall short. And I'm not suggesting that others shouldn't go ahead and sign up, or that they are in any way wrong to do so.

I just think that it's more in the true spirit of blogging not to ask others to conform to a single set of values but instead to trust our readers to form their own opinions about us, our politics and our own ethical code.

Guest post: David Cairns MP

Published: August 10, 2009

In the summer of 2009 I wanted to take a break from blogging and, following Iain Dale's example, decided it might be a good idea to invite parliamentary colleagues to contribute a guest post. This was by far and away the best of the bunch.

Tom has asked me to contribute a guest article for his on-line newsletter. As a neophyte in this niche, I looked around to see what the popular bloggists do. So here is the result: a pointless list.

It was either that or a fresh call for a Labour leadership contest, which would provoke a renewed internecine war within the party, but I thought you would rather have the list.

So, *a propos* of nothing at all, here is my considered opinion as to the five best and worst American presidents. From my extensive studies of the blogosphere it seems to matter what other people 'reckon', so please feel free to leave your reckonings in the usual place and Tom will paste them onto the newsletter as he sees fit. Or if you prefer you can write to me: c/o the House of Commons, SW1A 0AA.

David Cairns MP

THE TOP FIVE US PRESIDENTS

5. Thomas Jefferson

We all know the JFK quote, delivered to a room full of Nobel Laureates:

I think this is the most extraordinary collection of talent and of human knowledge that has ever been gathered together at the White House – with the possible exception of when Thomas Jefferson dined alone.

So Jefferson was brainy, (and Kennedy had good writers). But Herbert Hoover and Jimmy Carter were brainy too and look how that turned out. Brains alone don't make you a good President, (though they are kinda important, Sarah). His authorship of the Declaration of Independence, the Louisiana Purchase and his espousal of fine republican ideals ultimately outweigh his slave-owning and troubling relationship with Sally Hemmings.

4. Harry Truman

The patron saint of every unpopular politician; the man who left office more despised than Fred Goodwin with swine-flu, has been rehabilitated into one of America's best ever leaders (never going to happen, George). He specialised in taking incredibly difficult decisions – the bomb, recognising Israel, de-segregating the Army, spending billions to re-build former enemies, sacking General MacArthur – that were almost calculated to lose him popularity. Yet he trusted his mid-West instincts and his life-long study of human nature. He could have been dwarfed by the memory of his beloved predecessor but he had enough confidence in his own judgment and beliefs not to let that worry him. In the end, character matters, and 'Give 'em hell, Harry' had it by the bucket-full.

3. George Washington

Much though I admired Donald Dewar, the title 'Father of the Nation' really ought to be preserved for a tiny elite. (Mandela, I'll let you have it. You too, Gandhi.) General Washington wears the designation like he wore his old dress uniform: with under-stated but undeniable authority. He established the uniquely American quasi-office of 'nation's favourite General' (subsequently filled, inter alia, by Grant, Eisenhower, MacArthur, Schwarzkopf, Powell, Petraeus et al). Though better appreciated by the Americans than us – he did kick our butts after all – it can be hard to separate the facts from the hagiography. But he was clearly an inspiring military leader who eschewed the trappings of monarchy and set the pattern for a citizen presidency that lasted well into the twentieth century, but really exists in name only today. Shame.

2. Franklin Roosevelt

The revisionists are busy putting it about that FDR's stimulus package, the New Deal, actually prolonged the great depression, which is utter tripe, but handy for those do-nothingers – is that right Tom? – who oppose Obama's contemporary version, (a little bit of politics, ladies and gentlemen). From his wheelchair FDR towers over other twentieth century presidents, the only Chief Magistrate to serve more than two terms. Under Roosevelt the Democrats came to be associated with the progressive wing of politics, having been on the wrong side of most issues up to this point. He came to office in the worst possible economic climate and with an activist Supreme Court opposing him from the right, yet his vision, compassion and astonishing triumph over personal adversity make him the prime candidate for that un-sculpted bit of Mount Rushmore between cousin Teddy and Honest Abe.

1. Abraham Lincoln

No surprise here. My personal political hero. Over the years I have journeyed from Hodgenville, Kentucky, via Springfield, Illinois to Washington's Ford Theatre and the Petersen Boarding House trying to figure out this astounding, enigmatic man. Born in abject poverty to a semi-literate, subsistence farming father, a largely unschooled and lonely boy, he was driven by a ferocious ambition that ticked away like a little motor in his stove-pipe hat, as one contemporary put it. There is no doubt that under a lesser person (and we are all lesser people), the United States of America would have split in two. Enduring constant sniping from within his own cabinet, countless military set-backs, a hostile press, incompetent generals and a wife driven to the brink of insanity through grief, he never wavered from his belief that the American experiment in popular democracy should not be allowed to fail. He is the perfect marriage of high moral principle and low political cunning. On the downside, as a fan of Robert Burns, Lincoln would often recite Burns's long poems in 'a Scotch accent' (I know!). But he did free the slaves, so on balance we can forgive him.

THE BOTTOM FIVE US PRESIDENTS

5. Warren G. Harding

On the plus side, Harding died after just two years in office. The negative side is rather longer. A newspaper magnate, he secured the Republican nomination after ten rounds of voting on the grounds that he was 'the best of the second-raters'. His election was the first in which all women could vote, and they are believed to have supported him in large numbers partly on the grounds of his good looks (honestly, ladies). His corruption-ridden administration led the flight back to American isolationism after Wilson's noble, yet doomed, attempt to engage the country in the League of Nations. He died suddenly while on a nation-wide 'Voyage of Understanding', undertaken to re-connect the political classes with the general public. A lesson to us all.

4. Jimmy Carter

A Brazilian priest friend of mine once told me that when Jimmy Carter was elected, the army stopped killing people on the streets of Sao Paulo. That in itself should give pause for thought when listing the plain man from Plains, Georgia, as among the worst presidents. His post-presidency also stands out as the exemplar of how to use the prestige and moral authority of the office for good. Yet, in truth, he was never up to the job. Elected for his honest demeanour in the wake of the long national nightmare of Watergate, he made such heavy weather of governing that many believed that the job had simply become too big for any one person to do, until a certain B movie actor proved otherwise. Once he was attacked by that giant rabbit, it was all over really.

3. Ulysses S. Grant

A painful inclusion for me; Grant was the tactical genius who finally secured the Union triumph in the Civil War, after a run of generals who were amazingly reluctant to fight (Lincoln asked once if he could borrow the army if the generals weren't intending to use it). Grant almost stumbled into the presidency and was as hopeless at it as he had been at every other job he ever had outside the military. His administration became a by-word for corruption and incompetence, and though a few optimistic modern historians have had a bash at revisionism, it is unlikely that old Unconditional Surrender's occupancy of the White House will be remembered as anything other than a sad post-script to a towering military career.

2. Franklin Pierce

Historians like to debate whether the American Civil War was avoidable. On the one hand the sordid compromise over slavery in the Constitution was never going to hold, and sooner or later was bound to come to a head. On the other hand a whole series of terrible decisions were taken in the years leading up to the war that surely could have moved things in the right direction had they been taken differently. Pierce was the penultimate pre-war President and on his watch the Missouri Compromise was abandoned and the Kansas-Nebraska Act came into being, which made a bad situation very, very much worse. A drunk who sided with the Confederacy during the war, he will be remembered as the first President to come from New Hampshire; the other being Josiah Bartlett (can you check this, Tom? Ta).

1. James Buchanan

The nation's only confirmed bachelor-president, Buchanan became the Democrat candidate for the 1856 election when the party decided that no one could be any worse than Franklin Pierce, thereby establishing the Democrats' uncanny touch in candidate selection. He won the election against a divided opposition and then proceeded to do absolutely nothing for four years while the country fell apart around him. The concept of leadership, i.e., actually leading, was lost on Buchanan, who knew that disaster was looming but felt powerless to do anything to prevent it. He may even have had a hand in the worst decision ever handed down by the Supreme Court, the Dredd Scott judgment (certainly Lincoln suspected that he did), as he sought to avoid taking difficult decisions by having the court take them for him. By demonstrating a total abdication of responsibility in a time of unprecedented national peril, Buchanan runs away with the title of Worst Ever President.

Top ten tips for political bloggers
Published: February 10, 2010

I originally wrote this for the Young Fabians, who wanted a piece on 'Top Ten Tips for Labour bloggers'. But it could just as easily be aimed at bloggers of any political hue. It's now online as part of the Young Fabians' new 'Can The Internet Change Politics?' publication.

1. Politics is dull. Really, really dull. So when you write about it, you have to make it sound far more interesting than it actually is. And the only way of doing that is to be able to write well. A good writer can make just about anything sound, if not interesting, then not quite so dull.

2. Use humour. Political blogs, particularly left-wing ones, have a reputation for being very poe-faced and serious, because, like, politics is about people's lives, yeah? Don't take yourself or your politics too seriously – at least not all the time.

3. Go off-topic. Yes, readers will visit your site to read about politics, but it's okay to talk about other subjects occasionally. Even politicians and local activists have interests outside politics. Whether that's cooking or gardening or football or movies or … yes, *Doctor Who*. The key is to connect with your readers on a different level from the political one.

4. Don't go out of your way to criticise Labour, but don't be too worried about doing so either. Politics needs to be about debate, and one of the most regular – and valid – criticism of LabourList when it launched was that it was too on-message.

5. Allow commenters to have their say. By all means moderate the abusive ones, but blogging isn't one-way – a dialogue with readers is the life blood of a good blog. But conduct that dialogue on your own terms.

6. Update regularly. And I mean very regularly. At least twice a day, ideally more often. Your regular readers must understand that paying repeated visits to your site will pay dividends in terms of seeing new stuff.

7. Format and design is crucial. Narrow columns, an attractive, good-sized font with adequate spacing between lines makes it easier on the eye for readers who have an awful lot of other political blogs on their favourites lists all competing for their attention.

8. Blogging is a community in its own right and political differences, while still there, matter less, Be generous on your blogroll. Feature rival parties' blogs as well as those supporting your own.

9. Don't become a slave to the wordcount. If a post is worth only twenty-five words, write twenty-five words. Don't try to expand needlessly on a subject just to make it look better. Pithy can be attractive to readers who are in a hurry.

10. Synchronise. Use Twitter to publicise your posts, use your blog to promote your Twitter feed, use Facebook to send hugs to people you've never met. It's all good.

Top ten Twitter tips
Published: February 22, 2010

This turned out to be one of my most popular posts ever.

Having previously offered readers the benefit of my profound insights into the rules of political blogging, I thought those of you who use Twitter might be vaguely interested in this advice, aimed at politicians and candidates:

1. Don't just broadcast – engage. Politicians who use social media to let everyone know what they think but who

don't even respond to others' views are doing themselves no favours.

2. Do it yourself. I cannot emphasise this strongly enough: if you have a Twitter account, *never* let anyone else Tweet on your behalf. Without authenticity, your Twittering is valueless (at least, that's what I told Tom yesterday when I offered to write this for him…).

3. Don't Tweet and drink. Should be self-evident, but you'd be surprised how many are tempted. If you're out for a drink, don't even check your Twitter account for updates, lest ye be tempted to reply, however entertaining the results would be for the rest of us, and for the media (see numbers 9 and 10).

4. Argue by all means, but avoid being offensive. Respond with a pithy or sarcastic comment if you're provoked, but be more measured than your critics.

5. Avoid giving your diary details – nothing to do with security, it's just dull. 'Just had a very productive meeting with a really worthy organisation' might be of interest to members of that worthy organisation and to both of the constituents who follow your Twitter feed, but not to the rest of us. Also, avoid inane greetings and sign-offs: 'Morning Tweeps!' No one cares. Really, they don't.

6. Don't split your message over more than one Tweet. This is simply bad Twitter etiquette. The value of Twitter is in the discipline required to say what you want to say in 140 characters or fewer. If you want to write an essay, use a blog.

7. Tempting though it is to insist on getting the last word in a Twitter exchange, it's often more gracious to leave that to your critics.

8. Don't block followers. There are some real morons out there who get off on sending abusive Tweets, particularly to politicians. They wear the 'blocked by an MP' badge with pride. Far better to ignore them completely. Believe

me, that will annoy them far more than blocking
them will.

9. Always assume that whatever you Tweet will be read
by the news editor of the *Daily Mail*. Because that
assumption will be correct. Speak your Tweets out loud,
preferably to a third party, *before* you post. If you have any
doubts about whether it will be misinterpreted, then err
on the side of caution.

10. If you wake to find an army of reporters, photographers
and camera crews outside your home, it could be a sign
that you need to rethink your new media strategy.

And if I were in a sarcastic mood, I might just add an eleventh,
aimed specifically at the non-politician Twitterer:

11. Whenever an MP Tweets about buying anything, from a
mobile phone to a new sofa or car, reply along the lines
of 'You can always claim it on expenses!' This is always –
always – hilarious and will guarantee your status as the
Twittersphere's very own Oscar Wilde.

Virtual extortion

Published: April 1, 2010

*This one hooked in quite a few gullible readers as well. Check the
date, people!*

This week I tabled an Early Day Motion entitled 'Web Archiving
Provisions':

*That this House recognises the crisis in the internet community caused
by the rapid consumption of virtual memory; is nevertheless deeply
concerned at Government Clause 202 in the Digital Engagement Bill
which would, from April 2011, oblige website hosts to delete any*

internet content older than twelve months, forcing web authors to archive that material in advance; believes this poses a serious threat to web users' ability to continue to rely on the internet as a research tool; and believes that the Bill's provisions for forcing site owners to archive all material older than twelve months are draconian in the extreme.

It had attracted fifty-five signatures by the time I tabled it and I expect it to have more added by the time the Bill comes up for its Second Reading next Tuesday.

The new clauses, inserted by their Lordships last week when no one was looking, is a ridiculous over-reaction to the much-publicised fact that the internet's virtual memory is fast being used up due to the massive number of new sites being launched every day – particularly blogs. From a year today, everything older than a year, therefore, will be wiped – completely eradicated from the web in order to allow new stuff to be published online.

The plan is that anything older than a year can be archived by the owner and emailed on request to anyone wishing to read it. But what if we don't have the time or the inclination to do that? Well, the Lord Mandelson has an answer to that: the government will do it for us and charge us a fortune for the privilege!

I am reconciled to the inevitability of this site, from next April, only carrying posts dating back one year; for me and, I suspect, for my readers, that probably won't be a huge blow to our quality of life. But for other sites – the BBC and Wikipedia, for instance – it could prove calamitous. And what about those blogs that are much longer established than mine, like Iain Dale's or Guido's?

Wouldn't it be better simply to invest in more virtual memory for the web itself? The cost of doing so would be far less than what the Bill proposes – and infinitely more practical.

A fisking we will go…

Published: July 23, 2010

The term 'fisking' is apparently named after The Independent's *Robert Fisk, some of whose reporting on the Iraq war was analysed to bits by American bloggers.*

I've only met Will Straw once and he seemed a decent chap. But his latest pro-Lib Dem post over at Liberal Democrat Voice needs a bit of critical analysis.

Will should bear in mind, for a start, that the Lib Dems are sitting in coalition, propping up a right-wing Tory government, so I'm not at all sure why he thinks it appropriate to talk about the need for Labour and the Conservative Party's glove puppets to make up and be friends. But anyway, here we go…

Will says: 'I take no great joy in the spate of polls showing the Liberal Democrats in free fall.'

Why not? Come on, Will, it's funny! Better than most things on TV these days.

'The latest projections from UK Polling Report show that a Lib Dem collapse to 15 per cent in the polls would deliver a Conservative majority of eighteen.'

Indeed. Except there will not be an imminent general election. The Lib Dems may be about to shuffle off this mortal coil, but Labour – even a leaderless Labour – is still six points up on our (you can still say 'our', can't you, Will?) result in May.

'But the Lib Dems have not delivered on Nick Clegg's promise of a "fairer Britain"'

Well, duh.

'The Lib Dems in government have effectively capitulated.'

See previous comment.

'Meanwhile, the about turn on VAT and the timing and size of public spending cuts has been extraordinary.'

Yes, Will – they're Lib Dems! You did realise that, didn't you?

'With growth forecasts down, unemployment up, credit availability falling, but borrowing robust, he and his Cabinet colleagues are now giving cover for an additional £32bn of public spending cuts over this parliament. Worse, the cutting will start this year.'

But on the plus-side, they did get some shiny ministerial boxes, so, you know, swings and roundabouts.

'There is a temptation here for progressives, particularly those within the Labour Party, to look on from the side lines and allow the Liberal Democrats to dig their own grave.'

'Temptation' or 'moral obligation'?

'But this would be a mistake.'

No, it wouldn't.

'Progressives of both parties, and of none, must work together to support the Lib Dems in government to create a more progressive Britain.'

Not while the Lib Dems are supporting David Cameron, George Osborne and William Hague, they don't.

'Very little has actually been achieved so far.'

What about those shiny ministerial boxes? They've got leather handles and everything.

'But for those of us who supported the Liberal Democrats on their approach to climate change, constitutional reform and civil liberties, there is an incentive to help them.'

For those of us who supported the Labour Party against vicious and dishonest attacks on our party by Lib Dems, there is no such obligation.

'Both Lib Dems and Labour agreed in their manifestos on the need for electoral reform...'

Well, not really. At the fag end of the last parliament Labour reluctantly and ill-advisedly agreed to hold a referendum but didn't commit itself to campaigning for a 'Yes' vote.

'Whatever the electoral system we are likely to see more hung parliaments, rather than fewer, in the future.'

How so? Electoral reformers have been saying that since the formation of the SDP in 1981. Fortunately, they were wrong.

'Indeed, there has to be a reasonable chance that the 2015 election will make Labour the largest party in another hung parliament.'

But there must also be a reasonable chance that Labour will form a majority. And that's what we both want, isn't it, Will? Will? Hello...?

'Indeed, if polls are to be believe a Lib–Lab coalition may take place in Scotland next May.'

If polls are to be believed, Scottish Labour can form a minority administration at Holyrood in exactly the same way that the SNP did in 2007.

'The AV referendum is an interesting test case for this collaboration. Scupper it and the chance of a fairer voting system will be lost for a generation.'

Okay, we're singing from the same hymnsheet now.

'Both Labour and the Lib Dems should admit that the Conservatives are winning the argument across a range of issues at the moment.'

Well, the Lib Dems might be saying that because that's what the script from Conservative Central Office tells them to. But most Labour members think the government's making a mess of things. You want to spend more time with Labour people, Will.

'Within government, the Lib Dems must show more spine.'

But what about those shiny ministerial boxes? You know, with the leather handles and stuff? Wouldn't Dave take them away?

'In opposition, Labour must continue to expose the worst elements of the coalition's programme including its unfair approach to deficit reduction.'

And including its inability to implement that unfair deficit reduction package without the help of the Lib Dems.

'But they must also show a willingness to work together where there is common ground.'

No.

Extra-parliamentary activity

To the palace

Published: December 9, 2008

Carolyn and I are about to head off to Buck House to have a swift sherry with HM.

(I know, I know: first class travel, millions of pounds claimed in expenses, an on-site gym, subsidised food and drink, more nubile slave girls than you can shake a stick at and now an invitation to the palace! MPs have never had it so good; they should be taken out and shot instead, etc., etc....)

I'm not sure how often these events occur – the last time I attended was in 2002. I expect Carolyn will want to acquit herself with more dignity this time.

Basically, what happens is this: you mill around having a drink with a couple of hundred of your colleagues, then line up to meet HM and Prince Philip. Then after the formal introductions, various senior members of the household – last time that included the Queen, Prince Philip and Princess Anne – mingle with the guests. All very informal and relaxed.

Actually, now that I remember it, last time got off to a bad start. Carolyn and I shared a taxi from the Commons to the palace with Tory MP, Andrew Rosindell, famous at the time for his affection for his (very British) bulldog. At a loss for a topic of discussion, I asked: 'So how's the dog, Andrew?'

'He died.'

'Oh.'

I seem to remember the short taxi journey taking rather a long time after that.

Operation 'mystery shopper'
Published: May 21, 2010

During the election campaign I knocked on the door of a lady who told me of her concerns about Glasgow's methadone programme.

She said that large numbers of addicts who line up for their daily dose at a local pharmacy were making it extremely uncomfortable for ordinary residents trying to use the shop. The methadone users were abusive – to each other and to other members of the public – occasionally violent and always intimidating, my soon-to-be constituent told me.

I promised I would look into it. So this morning, accompanied by a member of staff, Donald, I waited outside the pharmacy in question before it opened. I wanted to see for myself if the disorderliness and abuse reported to me would actually materialise. I would go into the shop, iPhone in hand to make an audio recording of what went on. Then, having witnessed the problem, I would have a think about what to do next. This would, presumably, involve talking to the pharmacy owner, Greater Glasgow Health Board and perhaps even the local community police officers.

But first we had to get our stories straight; we couldn't just hang around the shop eyeballing the other customers for no apparent reason.

'Are you going to tell the owners you're the MP?' asked Donald.

'No, wouldn't want to admit that in public, obviously. Too embarrassing.'

'What will you tell them, then?'

'Dunno. Maybe I'll just say I'm there to buy half a dozen packets of condoms and a tube of Anusol.'

In the event, it was a damp squib. No queues of addicts, no shouting, no intimidation. Still, at least I went over there to see for myself. And if there's a next time, I'll probably lose the false moustache.

Government: better than the alternative

Prêts à prêcher

Published: February 21, 2009

I was unimpressed with the latest patronising initiative from the Department for Rural Affairs.

I remain unconvinced of the wisdom of telling our citizens, in the middle of a deep recession, that they shouldn't save money by buying cheap clothes.

Bafflingly, that seems to be the message from one government department.

The 'sustainable clothing action plan' is fine as far as it goes, and who can object to Tesco banning cotton garments made using child labour?

But the minister responsible, Lord Hunt, is quoted indirectly as saying that climate change is a bigger problem than the economy.

Perhaps, but only if you can afford it.

For the vast majority in this country, it *is* the economy, stupid. Most families are, quite correctly and justifiably, trying to make their household budgets stretch as far as possible. That will often mean buying cheaper clothing from some of the High Street chains.

People will be more inclined to worry about the effects on the environment of their shopping habits once they feel they no longer have to worry about how to pay for their shopping.

I'm far more sympathetic to the views of Jane Milne, business environment director of the British Retail Consortium, who said that these retailers should be 'applauded, not criticised, for providing customers with affordable clothing, particularly these tough economic times.

'They're raising standards for overseas workers, offering clothes made from organic and Fairtrade cotton and encouraging the re-use and recycling of unwanted clothes.'

If we're going to preach at people on this subject, we might as well tell people on low incomes that they should buy more expensive, organically-produced and free range food.

In other words, we shouldn't.

Pollwatch: Things can only get better, right? Right?!
Published: June 1, 2009

The unnamed colleague in the next post was David Cairns.

The following is a genuine exchange of texts in the last few minutes between a colleague and me:

Colleague: *Have you seen the new poll?*
Me: *Tell me.*
Colleague: *Con 40 Lab 18*
Me: *So you're saying it's not as good as others, right?*
Colleague: *I can see why you are regarded as one of the most perceptive political commentators around.*

Pollwatch: Oh, for ███ ███!
Published: October 10, 2009

A new ICM poll for the *News of the World* tomorrow gives the Tories a 19-point lead:

Conservatives **45** (+5)
Labour **26** (n/c)
Others **29**
I mean, what ███████ the ██████████ and I know exactly how ████████ ███████. But for that to happen ███████ ████ ██████████ would have to ███████ ████

and I don't ▮▮▮▮▮ see that happening unless ▮▮▮▮
▮▮▮▮.
▮▮▮▮ and ▮▮▮▮ but it's
▮▮▮▮▮▮ ▮▮▮▮ ▮▮▮▮
▮▮▮▮ ▮▮▮▮ ▮▮▮▮.
Honestly, I just feel like ▮▮▮▮ my ▮▮▮▮
▮▮▮▮ ▮▮▮▮ , which probably wouldn't help.

At least, that's my take on it.

A hung parliament: the worst of both worlds

Published: February 6, 2010

I hear that a *Sunday Telegraph* poll tomorrow will confirm the recent trend of predicting a hung parliament.

In many respects, this is good news for Labour, following so many months when our complete electoral obliteration was being predicted. Nevertheless, my blood runs cold at the very thought of a hung parliament, whoever is the largest party. The temptation and the pressure to begin horse-trading with the minority parties would be immense. And in the event of 'negotiations' between the Lib Dems and either Labour or the Conservatives, the party manifestos would be unceremoniously binned in favour of whatever lowest common denominators could be salvaged from the talks.

There have always been plenty of 'comrades' whose sole reason for campaigning to get Labour back into power after eighteen years of opposition seemed to be in order to give that power away to the minor parties. They wouldn't even need the excuse of a hung parliament to enter a coalition with the Liberals if they got the chance.

Those unfamiliar with the situation when Labour and the Lib Dems formed a coalition government at Holyrood should also acquaint themselves with the phrase 'the tail wagging the dog'. Because that's how democratic whatever form of proportional representation forced on the country by the Liberals would be:

the party that came third dictating to the biggest party – and the whole country – how it should govern.

Things seem to be moving Labour's way, and for me (and for the whole of the country, believe me) the best outcome will be a Labour overall majority. But if that were not achieved (and let me make it clear: I still think it can be) then it's important that whichever party forms a minority government isn't forced, through threats of votes of confidence by the main opposition party, into bed with Clegg (thirty-one is an uneven number, after all – Baboom! I'm here all week....)

New Lib Dem slogan's a winner!
Published: March 12, 2010

Their actual slogan wasn't all that dissimilar to this...

The Lib Dems have unveiled their general election slogan. I rather like it. It's pithy, catchy and down with the kids...

> **Building a fairer, prosperous Britain in a future that's working for equality for all and with really nice weather, innit? Oh, and did we mention proportional representation?**

The Lib Dem version of transparency: wait for the polls to close before offering an opinion
Published: March 14, 2010

Given what actually happened after 6 May 2010, you'll forgive me a degree of smug satisfaction at this post...

I'm not a fan of chick flicks, so I've not been watching Nick Clegg's speech to whatever conference he's speaking to this afternoon.

But I'll make a wild stab in the dark and guess that he's going to be no clearer on which party he would choose to support in the event of a hung parliament. David Laws, the Lib Dem MP, said on *Any Questions* on Friday that any such decision would not be taken until after polling day.

Thank you, David. Thank you for confirming what I've been saying for years about the undemocratic nature, not only of the Lib Dems but of their most precious policy – proportional representation.

It's entirely consistent of Laws to say that the public will not be consulted before the Lib Dems make a decision. That's the essence of PR: let the little people have their vote, then ignore what they say and start bartering away the very policies they voted for behind closed doors and without reference to them.

Refusing to come clean about which of the main parties the Liberals would support if they got the chance is the opposite of transparent and democratic. But it's entirely consistent for the Liberals.

If the Tories win...
Published: April 6, 2010

Whatever reservations I had about Gordon's leadership, I was in no doubt that his continued leadership of the country was far preferable to Cameron's. I was rather proud of this little bit of literary demagoguery, written on the day Gordon finally announced polling day would be on May 6. One colleague even asked if he could use it in his introductory leaflet.

If David Cameron becomes Prime Minister after 6 May, I warn you.

I warn you not to be old: I have watched the sneers on the Tory benches whenever they talk about the pension tax credit. I've seen them tut and roll their eyes whenever the winter heating allowance is mentioned. And I remember which party shattered the link between earnings and pensions, and which left office with record numbers of pensioners living in poverty.

I warn you not to be young: the Conservative Party have never supported the SureStart programme, they decry the tax credits which have allowed so many parents to go to work and raise their families out of poverty.

I warn you not to be gay: Chris Grayling.

I warn you not to get ill: the Patient's Passport on which every single Tory MP was elected in 2005 was a mechanism for transferring billions of pounds out of the NHS and into the private health service. Not only was this scheme devised by David Cameron, I have never heard a single Tory MP renounce it.

I warn you not to be a home or a business owner: interest rates and mortgage rates today are a fraction of what they were under the Tories.

I warn you not to use public transport: the Tories opposed the Act which made local bus services more accountable. And they have never stopped complaining about Labour giving free nationwide bus travel to senior citizens. They also think that profit-making train companies give too much money to the government, and should give less.

I warn you not to be a school pupil: far too many young people are becoming students these days, according to the Tories. Maybe they would prefer our children to go straight from schools to the factory floor, like in the good old days?

I warn you not to work for the minimum wage: because after years of opposing it, a Tory government would simply let it wither on the vine (and that's only if it survived another backbench attempt to abolish it).

I warn you not to care about climate change: the Tories are the sceptics' party of choice. Far too many Tory MPs would refuse to believe the scientific evidence to do anything about it.

I warn you not to have a job: Tory cuts ('the bigger and the sooner the better!') will deal a death blow to the recovering economy.

I warn you not to be an ordinary person, with an ordinary family, relying on local services.

If Cameron wins, be warned.

Lib Dems stare at their feet and wish their leader would shut up
Published: April 12, 2010

Nick Clegg suggested that the people of Britain would take to the streets in fury if we ended up with a minority government (in other words, a government that didn't include him).

I can see it now...

The nation has ground to a halt. Thousands of armoured police officers are ferried from place to place in attempts to quell the riots before they even start. There's evil in the air and there's thunder in the sky and a killer's on the bloodshot streets. Oh and down in the tunnel where the deadly are rising, oh I swear I saw a young boy... No, hang on – that was 'Bat Out Of Hell'...

But anyway, you can just imagine the rhythmic howls of protest, can't you?

What do we want?
An end to an electoral system that gives any one party an overall majority, however slim, with a minority of the votes!

When do we want it?
As soon as practicable, dependent on a referendum and the necessary parliamentary time to implement any change consequent from said referendum!

This is the dark vision of the future handed to us by none other than the Blessed St Nicholas himself, the leader of the Lib Dems. He's worked out that, even if there isn't a hung parliament, the winning party – whether Labour or Tory – won't have a large majority. And that would make people so gosh-darned furious that they would take to the streets and stamp their feet and everything, apparently.

In other words, the only result that will satisfy the violent thug lurking just under the skin of every seemingly normal, peace-loving British voter is one which ensures St Nick himself is sat round the Cabinet table. So don't say you've not been warned: vote Lib Dem or bad people will burn down your house.

Of course, not many will miss the irony of Clegg citing the recent unrest in Greece, given that many of that country's economic problems have their roots in its ill-advised decision to scrap its own currency in favour of the Euro. Now, remind me: which is the only party that remains unequivocally in favour of Britain going down the same route...?

Developments and observations
Published: May 10, 2010

I felt strangely detached watching the various reports of post-election bargaining, particularly one TV interview with Charles Kennedy who said that this kind of frenzied activity was the direct result of having a first-past-the-post electoral system. Presumably he meant that a proportional system of voting wouldn't result in post-election coalition negotiations?

I was extremely anxious that Gordon and his negotiating team were not allowed to draw up a deal with Clegg and then to present it to the Parliamentary Labour Party as a fait accompli. I had already said as much during the campaign to Tony Lloyd, the PLP chair, and expressed my concern that no PLP meeting had been arranged for immediately after polling day. Because of the new bonkers rules that parliament wouldn't meet for more than a week after polling day (in saner times it met the following week), there was a danger that without Labour MPs present at Westminster, the leadership couldn't be held to account for whatever they were prepared to give away to the Lib Dems. Eventually, lobbying by me and others paid off, and a PLP meeting was convened. But by then, the coalition deal had been done with the Tories.

What a day!

Okay, a few random thoughts…

1. The past few days – and especially today – have been the worst possible advertisement for PR. And before you leave a comment saying 'But this result was created by the existing first-past-the-post system', remember that this is the first time it's happened in nearly four decades; under most PR systems, we would be treated to this kind of circus after *every* election.

2. It's bad enough that the leader of the third-placed party has been given the power to appoint the British Prime Minister; it's utterly unacceptable that he now has power of veto over who leads the Labour Party. Once again, that's the kind of thing that would happen every time under most systems of PR.

3. I view the likelihood of a Lab-Lib-SDLP-Hermon-Alliance-DUP-SNP-Plaid Cymru coalition unlikely in the extreme.

4. It's reported that 'Labour' is offering the Lib Dems an immediate Bill to ditch FPTP in favour of AV *and* a referendum on further change afterwards. This cannot be delivered; Labour MPs will not support it. I do hope some senior Lib Dems are reading this.

5. The word 'progressive' has now been redefined as 'willing to barter away everything you campaigned for in return for the chance to be in government, albeit at the beck and call of a party that has spent its entire existence trying to wipe you off the political map'. Who knew?

6. I will support David Miliband for leader.

7. I wonder if Harriet will stand for the leadership and thereby create a vacancy for the deputy's job?

It could all have been so different

Published: May 13, 2010

There were some voices on the Left who demanded that Labour should bite the bullet and try to form a 'Rainbow Coalition' with every minority party in order to keep the Tories out. This offended my democratic sensibilities; surely the party that won more votes and seats than any other had the right to form a government, even a minority one? The SNP, who claimed that right after beating Labour by a single seat in the Holyrood elections exactly three years earlier, were nevertheless now espousing the principle that a coalition of losers would be a perfectly legitimate government.

I begged to differ, and went on various broadcast media to make my point.

The misjudgements and mistakes that felled a political movement

by Our Political Staff

As the dust finally settled on Britain's political institutions yesterday, the country began to review the events of the past twelve months and to estimate the colossal damage done to the central players in a drama which has bewildered and enraged the public in equal measure.

Senior Labour figures spoke openly of their anger and dismay, predicting with a glum confidence that their party is unlikely ever again to be entrusted with the responsibility of government.

It could all have been so different, as more than one former minister opined. Last week's general election need never have happened at all, the media pack was constantly reminded, had wiser heads in Labour prevailed following the previous election, nearly a year ago, in May 2010. If only Labour had refused to form the so-called (and short-lived) 'Rainbow coalition' in a desperate bid to cling onto power, the reasoning goes, then the electorate might have stayed their hand from the electoral slaughter to which Labour has now been subjected. Few pundits foresee a time when the party of Attlee, Wilson and Blair can hope to reclaim its role as one of the two major political parties in Britain.

So how did it come to this? How was Tony Blair's 400-plus parliamentary party transformed in fourteen short years into a third-placed rump of barely 100 MPs, elected by the votes of fewer than one in five of those who turned out?

The origins of Labour's demise lie in the aftermath of last year's election, when Nick Clegg was persuaded by his party colleagues to seek a coalition with Labour rather than the Conservatives, even though David Cameron's party had beaten both his rivals in both shares of seats and votes, though fell twenty seats short of a Commons majority. But the anti-Tory coalition that was cobbled together in the days after polling closed suffered from two major weaknesses from the very start: the first was arithmetic; even with the enthusiastic participation of the Scottish and Welsh nationalists, and the noticeably less enthusiastic support of the sole Green MP, Caroline Lucas, it gave Prime Minister Gordon Brown only a wafer-thin majority in the Commons. And when Lib Dem negotiator David Laws defected to the Conservatives within a week of the pact being agreed, that majority was effectively wiped out.

The second was Gordon Brown himself or, more accurately, his decision to announce his resignation as Labour leader – but not yet as Prime Minister – to facilitate a deal with the Lib Dems. Encouraged by David Davis's rejuvenated Tories, the media and large sections of the public howled their indignation at 'the stolen election'. To make matters worse, the head of the government was replaced four months after the election by a new Labour leader who, although elected in an open contest within the party, had not been chosen by the country at large. Constitutional experts pointed out that this was not contrary to the British constitution, but such arguments had little effect on public opinion, as polls showed Labour support falling below even the Lib Dems' freefalling numbers.

It was an unhappy polygamous marriage of convenience from the start. Labour promises of an immediate move on electoral reform had to be kicked into the long grass when Labour's 'awkward squad' refused to support any change without a referendum. Although Clegg and co. held their temper – and, for the most part, their tongues – Caroline Lucas did not. Her insistence that Labour replace its programme of a new generation of nuclear power stations with 'a windmill for every home' was scorned by Labour backbenchers and stonewalled by ministers. Her ostentatious march from the government to the opposition benches during Prime Minister's Questions at the end of 2010 remains one of the iconic moments of the shortest parliament in nearly forty years.

But it was Labour's decision to include the nationalists in their alliance which proved the downfall of the party and its government. It was hardly surprising that Alex Salmond, pulling the strings of his six-strong Westminster party from his Bute House lair, took great delight in systematically destabilising the very institution he had entered politics to destroy. His demands for a 'Barnett-plus' funding formula for the Scottish Parliament was widely assumed to have been demanded precisely because of its undeliverability. Similarly, his call for the removal of Trident nuclear submarines from Scottish territorial waters in return for his party's support for Chancellor Ed Balls's first budget had never been part of the original negotiations; it was conjured from Salmond's hat on prime-time TV just as whips were marshalling their forces for the vote, catching ministers off guard and resulting in an entertaining but confused and calamitous range of responses.

If stability really had been as important as Labour and the Lib Dems had insisted, the 'Rainbow coalition' would probably never have got off the ground. Instead of a secure government, the British public watched night after night as deals were agreed then dismantled, and agreements were reached then renegotiated – sometimes in the course of a single night. Parliament was reduced to a farce as the Conservative opposition used procedures and delaying tactics to run rings around embattled ministers who were never quite sure of the differences between the Opposition and the Enemy.

With virtually no achievements to its name, with a fragile economy and rising unemployment, with international markets registering their lack of confidence in the coalition, the drama reached its inevitable conclusion with a vote of no confidence in the government on Monday 28 March – precisely thirty-two years to the day since the historic vote that James Callaghan's government lost by a single vote, ushering in eighteen years of Conservative hegemony. Deserted by every one of his former allies (apart from the loyal and determined Lady Sylvia Hermon), David Miliband's unfortunate government lost by a slightly more substantial margin of seventy-two.

The consequent election brought a hammer blow to Labour's hopes of remaining Britain's second party; Prime Minister David Davis has embarked on the most right-wing government agenda since Margaret Thatcher's, with the official Opposition now led not by Labour, but by a Liberal Democrat.

Yes, it could all have been so different, the former minister complained. But regrets in politics are plentiful; the opportunities for correcting past mistakes are far rarer and incalculably precious.

Gordon must take his share of the blame for the coalition

Published: May 31, 2010

On Radio 4's *Any Questions?* on Friday, Toby Young said something I've been thinking – but not blogging – for a while: why didn't Gordon Brown simply resign as Prime Minister on the Friday after polling day when it became clear Labour had lost?

Is there any sort of precedent for a PM remaining in office after being beaten in an election in order to allow the Leader of the Opposition to start coalition negotiations with the third party? Surely the correct constitutional course of action would have been to accept the will of the people and to have tendered his resignation to the Queen, who would then have invited the Leader of the Opposition to form a new government. Without an overall majority, the decision as to whether or not he wanted to govern on his own or carve up a deal with the Lib Dems would have been Cameron's and Cameron's alone to make.

Had the Tory leader suddenly found himself heading to the palace on the Friday afternoon, before he'd even had a chance to open up talks with Clegg, the pressure from his party to form a minority administration would have been immense – possibly even irresistible. In which case, we would now have a vulnerable, unstable Tory government, able to govern but not legislate and poised for defeat at any time in the next year.

It's interesting that the watchword in the days after the election was 'stability'; the priority was to get a government that could govern with a majority for the long term. Well, maybe. But it seems to me that when the public elect a hung parliament, that means they hadn't quite made their minds up by the time polling day came around and that maybe they should be asked their opinion again in the near future after things settle down.

In the circumstances where a minority Tory government had to go to the country within a year, it's quite conceivable that a demoralised and skint Labour Party would again have gone down to defeat and that Cameron may have emerged with an overall majority. Perhaps an early second election would have produced a similar result to the first one, in which case a formal coalition would have been inevitable.

It's also possible that, with a new leader in place, Labour could have won an overall majority in the spring of 2011.

But by announcing he was staying in Downing Street in order to facilitate talks between the two other parties, Gordon acted, if not unconstitutionally, then at least in such a way as to inaugurate a new page in our constitutional setup. The ConDem coalition is the direct result of that action. We may, one day, come to regret bitterly this development and to wish GB had gone when the voters told him to.

As an American friend once told me: 'The British constitution is all very well in practice, but it would never work in theory.'

In defence of politics

The triumph of the anti-political classes
Published: April 20, 2008

Say what you like about Peter Oborne: he's a gent. After reading this post, he sent me a nice note (far nicer than I deserved, when you read the post) and a copy of his book. I still don't agree with him, mind.

Paul Staines points out that *ConservativeHome* have declared Peter Oborne's *The Triumph of the Political Classes* their chosen book of the year. Not having read it, I don't feel qualified to say something acerbic, like 'Ho hum' or whatever.

Nevertheless, Oborne's analysis is going to have to be responded to, for the sake of democracy. Because when journalists jump on this particular anti-politics bandwagon, they risk undermining not just the individual politicians they hate so much, but the very idea of representative democracy. When I hear right-wing libertarians talking about how awful every politician is, how we've all got our snouts in the trough, that we're not representative or – the worst possible accusation and the core theme of Oborne's book (I think) – that some of us are 'career politicians' who have spent our whole working lives in politics, I assume that the phrase 'the army could do a better job sorting out the country' is only a breath away.

This antipathy towards politicians itself isn't new. In fact it's been around for so long it's positively passé. But the sheer invective, the bitterness, the utter contempt, the downright hatred of people they've (for the most part) never met is new and corrosive. What's the end game? To drive the current generation of politicians out of the profession (and yes, it is a profession)? To be replaced by whom? By new politicians who will be different in every respect from what we already have? Or is the aim not to have us replaced at all after we've sloped off? A country run by Peter Oborne and Paul Staines? What a lovely thought.

I genuinely don't care about the opinion of people like that. But if their destructive philosophy permeates the public consciousness to any degree, and voter turnout consequently falls to historic lows, what then? Mission accomplished as far as Staines and Oborne are concerned, I suppose.

To be continued.

In praise of the House of Commons
Published: June 23, 2008

Received wisdom dictates that the House of Commons chamber is an anachronism; that its procedures and traditions serve only to exacerbate the gulf between the realities faced by citizens and the privileged, rarified environment in which their representatives operate.

MPs cannot refer to any other member using their name (unless quoting from an article) and instead must refer to them by their constituencies. An MP may refer to members who sit on the same side of the chamber as 'honourable friends', but to a member opposite as 'the honourable gentleman', 'the honourable lady' or simply 'the honourable member for (insert name of constituency)'.

And, of course, you must never EVER accuse another member of deliberately lying.

It all appears very quaint. But those who make the effort to listen to debates (and not just the bear pit that is Prime Minister's Questions) will, I hope, be impressed by the general standard of debate in the chamber. However esoteric or obscure the subject, the Commons will almost always produce some thoughtful consideration of it, on both sides of the House. And the debate will (almost) always be polite and courteous.

This last quality is of particular interest to me as a blogger. The constant criticism of PMQs (as the only Commons event with which most viewers are familiar) is that it's too 'Punch and Judy', that MPs on all sides are far too rowdy and badly behaved. So the general populace would prefer political debate to be more courteous and polite, yes? Well, maybe.

Many of the comments left on this blog in the last few days have been thoughtful and polite. Many of them have not been. It's the same with comments left on some of the better known blogs like Guido Fawkes and Iain Dale. What is it about the blogosphere that makes people believe they can address any other person in aggressive and offensive terms that they simply wouldn't consider appropriate in almost any other circumstance (certainly not face to face)? I can understand how anonymity might offer someone a chance to express views he or she might not want associated with themselves ordinarily. But does the fact that so many of those who leave comments choose to do so offensively mean that anonymity allows the real persona of the person writing to emerge? Or does it simply allow someone to adopt an invented, false personality to be discarded after temporary use? (And if you don't think I have a point here, check out any thread on just about any Scottish political story carried by *The Herald*.)

In the blogosphere, opposition has given way to hatred, argument to invective.

The age of deference is long gone, and good riddance. But have we thrown the baby out with the bath water? In abandoning deference (decades after we should have), have we also abandoned qualities like respect and politeness?

So thank goodness for the Commons. If continuing to treat with respect those with whom we disagree is seen by those watching as being out of touch, then thank goodness there's still one place in the land that is proudly out of touch.

How to reduce turnout

Published: August 1, 2008

Have we really thought through this 'votes at 16' issue?

On the only recent occasion when the Commons was given a vote on this subject – on a Ten Minute Rule Motion – I voted against. As a colleague at the time observed: 'I'll support votes at 16 when half a million 15- to 17-year-olds march on Parliament demanding it.'

In fact, I've had virtually no representations from constituents asking me to support this measure. It's one of those issues which, when put before people, will usually elicit a positive response. But it's certainly not an issue that young people, unprompted, will volunteer as an issue important to them.

And the reason all this is important is this: if 16- and 17-year-olds are to be given the vote, I worry that the most significant effect will be a huge increase in the number of 'voters' who don't.

I can almost hear the arguments winging their way towards me even as you read this: 'Why shouldn't they be allowed to vote when they can join the army/have sex/pay tax, etc?' (And I say 'they' rather than 'we' because this is a change which is almost invariably promoted by those who have already reached the age of majority, rather by those who might actually benefit from it.)

I think it rather unlikely that we will ever have a single age at which individuals attain all these rights. In the meantime, the argument for votes at 16 has not yet been made. If there are powerful arguments in favour, I haven't heard them yet.

But perhaps I will soon, because Labour's National Policy Forum has decided in favour, and it will now be put to national conference. It's a debate I'll be interested in listening to.

But just because something can be changed, it doesn't necessarily mean it should be.

Too much information
Published: January 7, 2009

The second paragraph of this post demonstrates my intuitive understanding of British politics.

So, the Information Commissioner has ruled that ministers can't have private meetings any more.

This is undoubtedly a cause of celebration for Lib Dem MPs who don't expect ever to be in government anyway. But at the risk (and for 'risk' read 'certainty') of being accused of being an anti-democratic control freak, there can sometimes be good reasons for holding private meetings where a record isn't taken. The most successful negotiations, between ministers and his civil servants, between departments or between a department and an outside body, can very often start with an informal discussion that, technically, didn't actually happen.

No more, apparently. Openness and transparency counts more than successful delivery of policy, I suppose. Hooray for the Freedom of Information Act and the Information Tribunal.

As a transport minister, I once received a request from the department's press office for details of the car I drive as a 'civilian', as it were. I informed my private secretary that, naturally, I wouldn't be divulging that information. But out of curiosity, I asked the press officer in question why he wanted the information. He said he had received a request from *The Times* for the make and model of the car each minister drove in their private lives.

Why should this information be divulged? What would be the rationale, I asked? Because if the department is telling people what kind of car to drive, their own choice of car was a matter of public interest, came the reply.

Two points of interest here: the Department for Transport doesn't tell anyone what kind of car to drive, and I certainly wouldn't have anyway. And even if that was something it did, I still wouldn't have dreamed of divulging that kind of thing.

I pointed out to the disappointed press officer that if we agree to give out details of the (non-government) cars we drive, the next thing will be a demand to know if we intend to take a long-haul flight when we go on holiday, or whether or not we have central heating installed in our homes. A flea in the ear was duly administered.

Of course, that particular piece of information was not applied for under FoI, but under MOPB (Minding Other People's Business). Still, given some of the recent rulings of the Information Tribunal, had it come under FoI, they would probably have sanctioned it.

In defence of the party system
Published: February 10, 2009

Shortly after the formation of the Scottish Parliament, I attended a seminar in Edinburgh that was examining the role of the different parties at Holyrood. At one point, a member of the audience asked: 'Why do we need parties at all? Why can't we just have 129 independent MSPs working for their constituents, not their parties?'

Most politicos present sighed at the gentleman's naiveté. Yet it's an appeal that's heard all too often. Politicians and others who consider themselves more politically sophisticated than the average member of the general public would do well not to sneer at such suggestions (as I did at the time, I have to confess); the disconnect between electors and elected has never been greater. It is recoverable, but not if we refuse to engage and meet these concerns head on.

Being an 'independent' MP is only superficially attractive. Yes, you're not answerable to party whips and you can attack, or support, any policy you wish publicly. But if you had 646 independent MPs in the House, and they were suddenly invited to take a position on any given subject, particularly a controversial one, they would line up for or against. And before you knew it – hey, presto! A party system.

And even if that didn't happen, general elections are not about electing 646 individual MPs to the legislature: they're about electing a *government* on a programme laid out in that party's manifesto. And once elected, those much-maligned whips have the job of making sure enough MPs vote in the right way to enable the executive to govern.

I'll make another confession: I have not, on every occasion, voted according to my own best judgement. It so happens that on the vast majority of occasions I happen to have agreed with my party and my government on whether a piece of legislation deserves to be supported or not. But there have been a handful of cases when I would rather not have voted a particular way, but did so for the sake of the government and my party (fortunately, so far, I've never had to vote for something which I fundamentally opposed in principle, though I don't rule out that happening one day).

And I did so, not because I would ever put my party above my constituents – if you believe your party's policies are at odds with your constituents' best interests then you're in the wrong party and you'd better do something about it sharpish – but because I believe parties can only govern if their MPs are disciplined. And yes, that often means compromise – but compromise in order to allow other, important things to happen, things that you hope and expect will benefit your and every other MPs' constituents.

Because politics is a messy business. At its best it can be uplifting and inspiring; at its worst, seedy and self-serving. Most of us find a respectable middle way that allows us to get on with the job and, ultimately, to do good, which is the main motivation for any of us, of all parties and none, to be here at all.

Unfortunately, we can't all be Mr Smith going to Washington or Westminster. But there is still enough good in the party system to allow any dedicated MP to avoid cynicism and defeatism.

Whatever weaknesses our existing political apparatus has, the party system of itself is not one of them.

In defence of the ministerial car
Published: February 22, 2009

They're at it again.

This time it's Ed Vaizey and Iain Dale who are donning the hairshirts on behalf of others by suggesting that the ministerial car is an unnecessary expense to the tax payer and should be abolished.

If you will permit me the conceit of quoting from my own words in the latest issue of *Total Politics*:

> There are some questions that politicians can ask the general public and be absolutely guaranteed an affirmative

answer. These include: do you think there are too many MPs? Do you think MPs should be paid less? Do you think MPs should have shorter recesses? Do you think MPs' pensions are too generous? Do you think MPs' allowances should be cut? You get the picture.

To which I could add: 'Do you think ministers should have their own cars and drivers taken away?'

It's such an easy, lazy hit, and I'm surprised that normally sensible Tories ('sensible' being a relative term, obviously) are indulging in the 'holier than thou' language normally reserved for Liberal Democrats. Of course you'll get the baying mob to agree with you, but just because something's popular doesn't make it right. If the Tories think that asking popular questions is the way to govern, then we're all in trouble if they do win next time.

As someone who no longer has a vested interest in the subject, I'm happy to defend ministerial cars. Ministers work ridiculously long hours, have to carry out all their ministerial duties on top of all their constituency duties and try, somehow, to fit in a family life as well. A car and driver makes life easier and, as Iain accepts, doesn't cost the public purse that much in the grand scheme of things.

Yes, a ministerial car is a perk. So let's hear it for perks! Because if you've just had a 12- or a 14-hour day and you're leaving the Commons after the last vote, it's wonderful to be able to slide into the seat of a car and relax while you're taken home, knowing you'll be lucky to get six hours sleep before your ministerial diary kicks in the next morning. I don't grudge that privilege to any serving minister and I wouldn't begrudge any future Tory minister, either.

But why draw the line at axing ministerial cars? Ministers also get paid extra on top of their MPs' wages. Why should that happen? In fact, while we're at it, why don't we just cut MPs' wages altogether?

This is such a silly, dangerous little game that (some, not all) Tories are playing, not because it endangers ministerial cars and the jobs of their drivers, but because it feeds into the anti-politics culture which the media is constantly encouraging. If the Tories ever do make it back to government, they will suffer just as much as Labour has.

Instead of thinking up gimmicks to catch the headlines, perhaps Tory MPs might start thinking about ... oh, I don't know ... some policies, perhaps?

UPDATE @ 8.01pm: As expected, most of the comments have supported taking away ministers' cars, reducing MPs' salaries, pelting all MPs with rotten fruit, etc. So no surprises, then. The logic seems to be: 'I don't have a ministerial car, so why should you?' Impeccable.

Here we go again...
Published: March 3, 2009

If I had known at the time that Iain Dale's company would one day be publishing this book, I might not have been so critical of him, fine chap that he is...

The decision by the Commons last night to change the rules on the publication of candidates' addresses has resulted in the predictable response from He Who Shall Always Be Holier Than Thou.

'Shameful', according to Iain. 'Naturally, MPs who don't live in their constituencies – and there are still plenty of them, believe it or not – will be delighted by this move.'

Dear me, Iain, were you pressed for time this morning and that's why you were unable to do a bit of research to find out what the amendment actually says?

If this amendment makes it into law, it will mean that all candidates standing at a general election will still have to tell the returning officer at what address they're registered to vote. That information would be checked, as it currently is, on the electoral register. The candidate would then have an option of having his home address printed on the ballot form or simply the name of the parliamentary constituency in which he is registered. So electors will still be able to tell if their preferred candidate is 'local' or not.

Iain might be surprised to discover that one of the reasons so many colleagues of both parties supported this is that many of us have young families who remain in the constituency home while we're in London. You may recall an incident recorded in Paul Flynn's book, *Commons Knowledge,* when a young woman, accompanied by her boyfriend, turns up at Paul's home while his wife and children are alone. The woman wants her MP's help in clearing her boyfriend of the charge of rape.

Without wishing to break any confidences, I can tell you that many colleagues have reported such incidents in the years since. In the weeks following the 2005 general election, Carolyn answered the door on two occasions to male constituents who were looking for me. They weren't at all threatening, but she didn't feel comfortable having to explain that at that moment, I was 400 miles away and she was alone with the babies.

The issue has become more worrying for MPs in recent years, because ballot papers are now posted in greater numbers to voters' homes; there is a far greater opportunity to take note of the information contained in them now than there ever was when the only time you got the chance to peruse the ballot paper was for a few seconds in the polling booth.

So all candidates, including MPs standing for re-election, will still have to give the returning officer exactly the same information they do at present (the only check that's ever been made, incidentally, of where a candidate lives. Such procedures, of course, will never be enough for those who feel it is their duty to sit outside an MP's home with a pair of binoculars, a notebook and a box of doughnuts.) And electors will still be able to know if any candidate lives in the constituency in which he's standing.

But why should anyone pay attention to the concerns of these bloody women and their young children, eh? If they didn't want to be abandoned for most of the week, they shouldn't have married an MP. And it's not as if there have been any actual cases of assault or harassment of MPs' families, so why should we change the law just to make them *feel* safer? And surely their insecurity is a small price to pay for the right of the public to know the actual street name and house number of their MP?

I think that's how the argument goes, isn't it, Iain?

Agree to disagree. Then call the police...
Published: March 28, 2009

Remember the days when politicians and journalists would trade arguments?

Ah, happy days! Nowadays, it's difficult to open a newspaper (and impossible to browse the blogscape) without reading about the latest threat to imprison political opponents. Simon Heffer is the latest to indulge in this tosh. In today's *Telegraph* he writes:

> It would be a brave person who sought to argue that what Mr Brown has done, and what he is now pressuring Mr Darling to do, is not a wholesale act of criminal negligence. Simply losing the next general election is, frankly, not enough of a punishment for a man who has inflicted such damage on our country that people won't even buy government bonds any more. An example needs to be made of him. I want him behind bars.

I'm sure Heffer's sentiments will find an echo among many of my own readers (though not, thankfully, among most of my voters). There's a distinctly unpleasant edge to much debate today which has more resonance in the political culture of certain South American countries than here in the UK. 'You disagree with me? I'll put you in prison!'

In the States, the Republicans' knee-jerk reactions to losing elections is to impeach Democrat presidents. Like many fashions, it has crossed the pond. The term 'impeachment' has never been widely used here, but it carries overtones of the much more glamorous American system and so some politicians from the minor parties started using it when they attacked Tony Blair over Iraq (however, one of those minority party politicians, Alex Salmond, once got into difficulty when debating Iraq with me on the radio: he claimed that Richard Nixon had been impeached and that Bill Clinton had not. I pointed out that it was the other way round. Alex was assuming, like many people, that 'impeachment' is the same as 'conviction'. It's not.)

So, from the *Guardian/Independent*-reading middle-class wet dream/fantasy of trying Tony Blair with war crimes on the basis that they didn't agree with his foreign policy, we now have the right wing, in the shape of Heffer, demanding not that Labour are thrown out of office and into opposition, but that the Prime Minister should be imprisoned because they disagree with his economic policy.

Is this what it's come to? That political debate isn't enough to engage the public anymore, so we have to up the ante and start threatening the individual liberty of political opponents? You can see where this is headed, can't you? After all, death threats are perfectly acceptable if you think the local government settlement this year isn't going to allow council spending to keep pace with inflation…

Alternatively, how about this: we have a political debate about the issues between now and the general election, then we vote, and whichever party wins, forms the next government. Radical, yes?

Meanwhile, let's lock up Simon Heffer (only joking, of course…).

Let's hear it for party politics
Published: June 2, 2009

Believe me, it is very difficult these days to try to motivate party activists to go out door-knocking, and I know this is not a problem confined to the Labour Party.

Party membership, and particularly party campaigning, is a voluntary activity. Those who join and want to get involved at a local level in the Labour or Conservative or Lib Dem parties do so for mostly altruistic reasons: they want to make a contribution to making things better and they feel they can do this by promoting the policies of one particular party. They give up a lot of their spare time to sit in drafty community centres of a Thursday evening, listening to councillors give long and detailed reports while others are sitting comfortably at home with their families watching telly.

Party activists make sacrifices – of their time, their money, their shoe leather and their patience. And in the last few weeks many of them will be wondering why they bothered.

This Thursday will be a difficult day for Labour, according to all the polls. But it will also be bad, to a greater or lesser degree, for British politics.

But here's the truth: after all the scandal and the dishonesty and the resignations and the refusals to resign, the indignation and the public fury ... after all that, politics is still worth the candle. I would today still urge young people not just to become involved in 'politics' – which is too often shorthand for a non-party campaign or movement – but to join a political party, to work for a candidate and yes, to become a candidate themselves one day, even to become a Member of Parliament.

Because that's still the best way to make a political contribution, even with all the compromises and concessions that are necessarily a part of party politics and which have always been intrinsic to it.

As for Labour, I still fervently believe that we deserve the public's support more than any other party. At both local and European level, we have shown that we have the individual talent as well as the policy and agenda to make things better for the people of this country.

Please vote on Thursday. British politics can deliver and it deserves another chance.

And vote Labour.

Proud to be an MP

Published: July 29, 2009

This was written in the immediate aftermath – and in response to – the MPs' expenses scandal of 2009.

I was twenty years old when I decided that I wanted to devote my life to politics. For me that didn't just mean having the ambition to be elected one day as an MP; it meant wanting to make a contribution to the benefit of my country.

That sounds pompous, doesn't it? I agree, it does. But it was and is true, so I don't care.

The men and women I work with, people from different parties, are some of the best individuals I've ever had the privilege to meet or work with. Some of those people, the ones I describe as among the 'best', were fingered in the Great Expenses Scandal of '09. Nevertheless, my and others' respect and liking for them remains. Many who were caught up in that exposé have decided to call it a day at the next election, as have many others who emerged from the episode relatively or entirely unscathed.

That is a matter of great regret, for me as well as, I suspect, for them. The House of Commons is not a den of thieves, of 'troughers', to use one of the less imaginative and attractive epithets in common usage. I can put it no better than Tony Blair did in his last appearance at the despatch box on 27 June, 2007:

> Some may belittle politics but we who are engaged in it know that it is where people stand tall. Although I know that it has many harsh contentions, it is still the arena that sets the heart beating a little faster. If it is, on occasions, the place of low skullduggery, it is more often the place for the pursuit of noble causes.

Those comments, of course, were made before this year's expenses scandal. I wonder if Tony would still have made them if the scandal had come first? I hope he would have, because they are as true today as they ever have been.

There is no shortage of those who want to disparage politicians and politics. They are wrong. But it is difficult to make a case for politics in the current climate. That doesn't mean we shouldn't.

Because politics is a noble and honourable pursuit. It was so at other times in our history when the public and the media held us in contempt. As I'm fond of reminding interviewers, when the Houses of Parliament burned to the ground in 1834, a crowd gathered on the other side of the Thames and cheered. Colleagues who fret that public esteem of politicians is at a dangerous low should bear in mind that, although it's necessary to try to improve public opinion, they should manage their expectations; politicians have always been despised. We will always be despised. Sometimes the degree of contempt waxes and wanes throughout the years and through events. But we will never be loved. That is not why we're in public life.

We are in public life because, as I said at the start, we want to make a contribution to the benefit of our country, to the condition of our fellow citizens. Every single MP I know does that in his or her working life every week; we communicate, we ask questions (of our constituents as well as of ministers), we lobby on behalf of the people we represent and, on far more occasions than we're ever credited for, we help people. We make a positive difference. We do good and we work hard doing it.

Those are the realities of life as an MP. We're not saints nor should we be. Neither are we villains. We're ordinary people who have been given an extraordinary opportunity.

There have been points in recent weeks when MPs have felt less than proud of our vocation (or profession, if you prefer). I've even felt the need to apologise to those who ask me what I do for a living. And I was wrong, because there is no reason to apologise for being an MP, of being chosen by your party and then your constituents to perform an important job.

One colleague, the day before the House rose for the recess, asked some of us, in all seriousness, how we would respond if asked by people we might meet on holiday what we do for a living. It was his genuine concern about the anticipated negative reactions to his mumbled, apologetic confession of 'I'm an MP' that inspired me to write this post. Because my colleague is a good guy. He should be proud of who he is and what he does.

I will never again be reluctant to advise young people in my local schools to go into politics. If you want to make that difference in people's lives, in the life of our nation, there's no better way — there's no *alternative*, in fact — to taking a deep breath, holding your nose (if you feel you must) and taking the plunge into party politics. I will, however, advise them to avoid it unless they know they can develop a thick skin.

There. That's what I think. I should have said it long ago. Do your worst.

Cameron: 'I f***ing hate politicians'

Published: September 10, 2009

I was becoming increasingly frustrated by senior colleagues jumping on the anti-politics bandwagon – a silly and lazy thing to do. And if you also happen to be a multi-millionaire it's quite easy to say we should stop low-paid parliamentary researchers from being able to buy cheap food in the Commons canteen.

Politicians will rue the day they were born if the Conservatives get their way, David Cameron promised yesterday.

Announcing a series of reforms to be implemented by a future Tory government, Mr Cameron said that MPs were 'the lowest form of life known to man' and 'utter scum'.

The Tory leader said that his government would not only cut the number of MPs by 'at least' 100 per cent, but would also make sure their salaries were cut radically, forcing them 'to depend on their trust funds like ordinary people'. He also promised to raise the cost of food and drink in the Palace of Westminster and suggested that staff might want to spit in MPs' tea, 'just to remind them who's boss'.

'I'm so glad I never went into politics,' Mr Cameron told a room packed full of journalists and a scary-looking bloke in an anorak and clutching a thermos flask who said he was from the Tax Payers' Alliance.

Asked what qualities he hated most in politicians, Mr Cameron replied: 'Cynicism and populism.'

Politics is not a dirty word
Published: January 5, 2010

I love politics. It fascinates me. I expect you feel the same, otherwise you wouldn't be reading this book.

So the general election campaign has started already, eh?

How will the public put up with the constant policy announcements, rebuttals, prebuttals and arguments between now and polling day, whenever that is? Best subscribe to Sky Movies for the duration or go abroad for a few months, blah, blah, etc., etc....

Are our 'humorists' and cartoonists, let alone our political commentators, even capable of doing anything other than rehashing these tired old clichés? Oh, how awful it is to live in a democracy and to be given a choice about who forms the government! And how dare the government and opposition parties interrupt our daily diet of *Big Brother* and *Celebrity Soap Stars Do Their Washing Up* or whatever, just so that they can explain what they would do with the reins of power in the next five years...

Don't enjoy politics? Tough. I can't stand football, but I still have to sit through sports 'headlines' interrupting proper news bulletins every day.

Yes, politics and politicians have a terrible reputation, and it's worse since the expenses scandal. But it was bad before then and it always will be. We can't blame the media exclusively for our reputation; our own behaviour has brought us to this place. But the media's constant and unimaginative carping about the negative aspects of politics does the whole country a disservice.

Maybe democracy is a rubbish way of running a country, but as Churchill said, it's better than all the alternatives.

What's even more infuriating is that the same commentators who spend their whole time describing politics as dishonest and boring and who describe politicians as venal and narcissistic, are the same people who, after polling day will scratch their heads and wonder why turn-out was so low.

The post-democratic era?
Published: January 26, 2010

I still consider this one of the most important and true posts I ever wrote.

Some will call this gross cynicism from a politician; others will call it defeatism. But let me ask a question: does it really matter all that much if the public feel less of a duty to vote now than in previous years?

There are, of course, some who 'positively' abstain from voting for various reasons: distrust of politicians and a lack of faith in our electoral system adequately to represent voters' preferences being two of the main ones.

But there is a far more fundamental – and for some, more worrying – factor behind low turnouts in recent general elections: apathy. That may not sound like a profound insight, but I'm not talking about apathy borne out of disillusion with politics; I'm referring to non-voters who not only have no interest in politics but who have never, in their adult lives, felt the need to be interested in politics. It's not that they hate politicians or politics per se; it's more the case that they've never seen the point of politics, and anyway, they've got more important things to be getting on with.

For people who read, or even comment on, political blogs, who look forward to general elections, who actually know who their MP is and which party he represents, this attitude is entirely alien. But to a growing section of society, that level of political engagement and awareness is just as peculiar a concept.

There are a number of reasons why I fear the trend towards political disengagement may not be reversible.

The post-war generation grew up in a country that still vividly remembered that its very survival depended on collective action and a sense of community. Voting was a duty and democracy a hard-won right which parents and grandparents had fought and sacrificed to preserve. But over the years that generation has been steadily replaced by one which became increasingly individualistic; society, nation and community were relegated in terms of importance, while the individual moved to the top of the list of their priorities.

The 'instant gratification society' is partly to blame: the internet has instilled in us an expectation that if you want something, you should get it instantly. Remember the days when, instead of downloading a podcast of your favourite radio show or watching an episode of your favourite TV drama on BBC iPlayer, you had to check the TV listings and then make sure you were in your house and tuned into a particular station when it was broadcast?

Remember when, if you wanted to buy a particular song, you either recorded it off the radio onto a cassette or physically went to a shop and bought the single? Today we take it for granted that if we want to own any song, we can download it in seconds.

Remember when you had to wait for the next TV or radio news bulletin in order to catch up on current affairs? Now, breaking news appears in real time on your desktop.

Why should we have to face the inconvenience of waiting? For anything?

So it's hardly surprising that a growing number of people can't quite get their heads around the idea of a political party promising to fix the economy, the health service, the schools system, in a timescale of years. Years? Are you mad? This is Tuesday already – we need solutions by tomorrow at the very latest...

On top of that, there's the apathy trap. I've met young-ish people in my constituency who are quite glad to see me coming round their doors asking for their support, who show no obvious hostility towards me or my party, but who seem a bit puzzled by the idea that they should be thinking about who to support in the general election. Often their parents never voted either. Now, when I was growing up, my parents always made a big deal about voting on every possible occasion. They would discuss when they would walk up to the polling place together, after they both got in from work, they would talk about whatever election was happening in a positive way. So by the time I was eighteen, I was champing at the bit to do the same, to do my civic duty.

But in talking to some of these non-voters over the years, I've come to the conclusion that some of them are even a bit nervous about the whole process of going to vote. That will sound absurd to some. After all, what could be simpler? But some people I've spoken to, who have reached their late twenties or early thirties and who have never been encouraged to vote because none of their families or friends do either, seem to view the prospect of voting with some trepidation. One young woman I spoke to was quite up front about her fears that if she turned up to vote she might humiliate herself by not knowing what to do.

All of this points to the uncomfortable conclusion that, despite occasional upward blips in turnout (2010 will be higher than any of the previous three elections because it will be seen as a tighter race than any since 1992), the historical trend is downward.

But does it matter?

Turnout in local elections has been regularly below 50 per cent for as long as I can remember. Same with European elections. Even in Scotland, significantly fewer voters bother to vote in Holyrood elections than in UK general elections. Has this meant that politicians elected on these occasions have had less of a democratic mandate?

No.

For all the above reasons, I fear we are living in a 'post-democratic' era. Fewer and fewer people are voting or joining political parties or trade unions. In one sense that's a disaster for the body politic. But perhaps we should instead look at this phenomenon, if not in a positive light, then as an inevitable consequence of a more individualistic, wealthier society where most people have historically large amounts of disposable income but who spend longer at work. And with less quality time to spend with their friends and families, and more money to spend in that time, they find their priorities are quite radically different from those of their grandparents. It would be odd if that were not the case.

This is why I have, in general, been dismissive of those who bang on about constitutional change as a way of 're-engaging' the public. If someone has decided, albeit passively, to opt out of the democratic process, they're not going to change their minds because we have a new electoral system or because the House of Lords is to be elected instead of appointed. Those issues simply feed the obsessions of those who are already involved and who, frankly, sound, to increasingly large numbers of ordinary (non) voters, like they're speaking a foreign language.

Where does that leave those of us who do want to engage, to vote, to comment, to join? Well, potentially, it gives us a lot more influence. If, ten years from now, 50 per cent fewer people are voting, then your individual vote will be twice as influential as now.

Okay, you're right – that *is* unconscionably cynical…

Hate mail

Published: April 15, 2010

The reference to being a 'former' parliamentarian is a nod to the technicality that once parliament is dissolved for a general election, there are no longer any MPs. I wasn't planning on resigning or anything.

The middle of an election campaign is probably the wrong time to start criticising your electors. And in my defence, only a tiny number of the 68,000 people I have represented as MP for Glasgow South are in my sights on this one.

Yesterday, I received an abusive email from someone claiming to be a voter in Glasgow South, though she refused to divulge her postal address, so I can't confirm this to be the case. Having recently discovered this blog, she was clearly unimpressed:

> While fully appreciating everybody is entitled to time off to relax and pursue hobbies and interests, including MPs, I did find it all too typical of our parliamentarians that you devote so much time to discussing *Doctor Who* and karaoke nights when this country is suffering from the worst economic crisis since the Depression. No one is denying you leisure time, but surely there are man [sic], many more important matters to mention, such as job losses, crime, education, the plight and traumas suffered by our soldiers and their families, who have been so horribly affected by the wars in Iraq and Afghanistan.

I know I shouldn't rise to the bait, I know, I know, I know... But let's just have a look at what she writes.

'While fully appreciating everybody is entitled to time off to relax and pursue hobbies and interests, including MPs...' Really? You fully appreciate that I'm entitled to time off and to pursue hobbies and pastimes? Excellent. We don't have a problem then, do we?

But then: 'I did find it all too typical of our parliamentarians that you devote so much time to discussing *Doctor Who* and karaoke nights.'

Setting aside for the moment her odd claim that being a fan of *Doctor Who* and karaoke is 'typical of our parliamentarians' (it's really not, you know), the charge seems now to be that my pastimes and hobbies don't meet with her personal approval. Unfortunately, she hasn't included in her email a list of 'approved' activities.

Of course, as a blogger and as a (former) parliamentarian, I do discuss more serious political issues, including our foreign wars and the economy. If she had had a look at my parliamentary website she would have read about my pledge to support our armed forces. And if she had read the 'About me' section of this site, it might have persuaded her not to reach immediately for the green ink. The thing is, I do try to make this blog reflective of my personal as well as professional life, and I do not spend all my free time considering weighty matters of state.

I work hard. I work hard as an MP because I think it's an important job and that the people I represent deserve to have someone who will do everything he can to help them. I'm working hard as a candidate because I think every single vote is worth fighting for, regardless of how 'safe' any seat is perceived as being.

But I also have a family, I have interests outside politics, I have friends I like to hang out with, I like to watch movies and TV programmes. That includes *Doctor Who*, but so what? If you don't like it yourself, I have a solution: don't watch it. The same solution suggests itself to those who don't enjoy my blog. I strongly suspect that if I were a football fan and spent two hours every Saturday watching two dozen blokes running aimlessly round a field somewhere, that would inexplicably be seen as a more acceptable interest for an MP to have.

And I like to blog. If any (former) constituent wants to complain that I have not been carrying out my duties as an MP, then I will take that seriously. However, this particular woman's complaint seems to be that I actually have some spare time, or that my spare time shouldn't be 'spare' at all, that it should be devoted to my job (hence eliminating the 'spare' from 'spare time').

The same email describes me as:

> extremely egotistical, a publicity seeker, pompous and self-serving.

I'm taking a wild stab in the dark here, but if she is a voter in Glasgow South, I suspect she may not support me.

Telly

A difficult truth for would-be superstars

Published: August 16, 2008

Having thoroughly enjoyed the opening episode of *The X-Factor*, I'm nevertheless reminded of the same reservations I've had during each of the previous seasons.

Every week of the auditions, almost every candidate tells the cameras that he/she wants nothing more in their lives than to be famous; they want to be more famous than Mariah Carey or Madonna; they want to sell more albums than Robbie Williams. The level of self-belief is startling, particularly given the limits (of most) of their singing talent.

Prince Charles got a lot of stick a few years ago because he said that young people should have more realistic ambitions. He was criticised by, among others, the then Education Secretary Charles Clarke, who interpreted Charles's remarks as a 'know your place' put-down from the upper classes.

It was nothing of the sort. I remember thinking at the time that HRH was spot on. A frighteningly high proportion of young people want only to be celebrities. More importantly, it seems to me that they want to be famous more than they want to be famous *for doing something*; celebrity is everything.

Telling those young people that their dream will come true if they really believe it will, and if they want it enough, is bordering on cruelty. It's certainly irresponsible, because the fact is they're not going to be singing stars.

One woman on tonight's programme is a case in point. A mother since a very young age, with a history of drug abuse, she said she wanted to give her children a new life and she was clearly sincere. But she also said that she didn't want to do anything except sing. Now, as it happens, she gave an outstanding audition and I wouldn't be surprised if she got down to the last two or three. But what if she doesn't realise her dream? What of the hundreds of thousands of young people who, if not actively encouraged, aren't exactly discouraged from focusing every ounce of their energy to attain an unattainable dream?

A couple of weeks ago, Michael Gove criticised the publishers of magazines like *Zoo* and *Nuts* for peddling an unrealistic view of women. More damaging, surely, to young people's self-esteem are those magazines which treat celebrities as objects of worship and respect, even where the reasons for achieving celebrity status is either unclear or disreputable. 'You, too, can have all this,' these publications seem to be saying. 'All you need to do is win a reality TV show.'

Which is why I'm such a fan of Simon Cowell's. His role as the hard man of the judge's panel on *The X-Factor* is, I'm sure, largely a media construct. But when he tells auditioning hopefuls that they should give up their dreams of becoming singers, that they don't have the talent to make it, he's offering them advice that their families and friends should have given them a long time ago.

There's nothing wrong in having dreams or even in having a go at realising that dream. But when reality bites, it's time to use your talent for something more achievable.

So that's that off my chest. Now I can get on with the traditional run-up to Christmas in the Harris household: tuning into *The X-Factor* every Saturday between now and December.

Grabbing our attention by behaving like a spoiled brat

Published: December 31, 2008

What a spiffing wheeze, those oh, so talented and clever Channel 4 executives must have thought.

Have Mahmoud Ahmadinejad, that well-known Jew-hater and president of a nation that funds terrorist attacks on British troops, give the alternative Christmas message! Fantastic idea!

'And yet,' those young, daring tribunes of free speech must have thought, 'doesn't this pose a moral dilemma for us?'

And of course, it does: after all, how on earth will Channel 4 be able to trump this next year? Having offended so many people in one fell swoop, who can they book for the Christmas Day 2009 slot who will offend even *more* people? Assuming Osama bin Laden's agent still isn't passing on messages, who can they get? Peter Sutcliffe, perhaps?

And no, I'm not making an attack on free speech; I'm not suggesting Channel 4 should not have the right to book anyone they want for their silly little self-indulgent three o'clock slot. I'm merely exercising my own right to freedom of speech by suggesting that offering a platform to someone who thinks Israel should be wiped off the map, and whose country actively funds Islamist terrorism, is disloyal to one's own nation and amazingly irresponsible.

But hey, that's Channel 4 for ya – irreverent and whacky, those rascals will just keep on 'challenging our preconceptions', as they themselves might describe it.

The rest of us would probably prefer to call it pathetic attention-seeking.

Don't sack Jeremy Clarkson

Published: February 6, 2009

I had promised myself I wouldn't write about this subject, but it's difficult to avoid.

Of course he shouldn't have used such offensive language to describe anyone, least of all his Prime Minister, and especially not when he was in another country. Clarkson used the terms 'Scottish' and 'one-eyed' as insults, and as someone who is the former and whose father is both, I do find his remarks offensive.

Nevertheless, I won't be filing a complaint. As I've said before, no one has the right not to be offended, and I'm getting heartily sick of the siren calls for sackings every time some attention-grabber grabs some attention by saying or doing something deliberately (and occasionally accidentally) shocking.

It makes me wonder if the only resort we now have against unpalatable opinions is to deprive the culprit of his livelihood. Whatever happened to reasoned debate or, as would be more appropriate in Clarkson's case, derisive mocking?

How to survive the inevitable zombie holocaust

Published: July 31, 2009

When, in 2009, And Another Thing… *was voted the best MP's blog in the* Total Politics *Blog Awards, pushing John Redwood's Diary to the Number 2 spot, John responded online with his customary good humour and grace. Well, okay, he didn't at all. He wrote something along the lines of 'Maybe if I wrote more posts about* Doctor Who *or how to survive a zombie holocaust, I would have been voted Number 1…' Yeah, maybe, John.*

This week I took advantage of Carolyn's short absence from home to watch Charlie Brooker's excellent *Dead Set*.

There have been so many zombie movies in the last three decades and it has clearly proved difficult for writers and producers to come up with new angles on a well-worn theme. Brooker's novel approach involved placing the action on the set of *Big Brother* (mindless mobs outside the gates blindly craving the delights contained within that famous studio: geddit?).

But there are quite a few consistencies (I won't call them clichés) when it comes to the-dead-coming-back-to-life-and-eating-living-flesh scenarios. This seems to me an interesting phenomenon – a symptom of the communal human 'hive mind', if you will, when Great Truths of Humankind become part of the mass subconscious. Hence, we know simply by instinct that when the zombie holocaust – or Zomfest – arrives, our survival will depend on a number of factors:

1. Are the dead returning to life as 'runners' (as in *28 Days Later* and *Dead Set*) or as 'walkers' as in *Shaun of the Dead* and George A. Romero's classic 'Dead' series? (And further to *28 Days Later*, memo to self: must write blogpost about films that everyone thinks are great but are in fact totally rubbish.) This is clearly of the utmost importance; however 'menacing' a slow shamble might look on the big screen, it's a hell of a lot easier to deal with than a resurrected Linford Christie.

2. Are the re-animated seeking living flesh (*Dead Set, Night of the Living Dead*) or are they being more picky, specifically going after the *brains* of the living (*Return of the Living Dead*)? If they're settling for dead corpses, you're in luck: there'll be plenty of dead neighbours/colleagues/family members lying about to act as diversion bait. On the other hand, if they're after human brains and you happen to be stuck at Conservative conference, you're *really* in trouble (wah-hey! I'm here all week, etc...).

3. Is the zombie virus spread by bites alone or by blood infection (*28 Days Later*)? If the latter, you really are in trouble. But then, if you're facing a plague of the living dead, then it's all degrees, isn't it?

4. Is the government/army on your side? This is a crucial one and will, of course, depend on whether the government inadvertently started the zombie plague in the first place through an accident while attempting to weaponise a virus or whatever. Politicians, eh? What are they like? And bear in mind that the government's solution to ... er, 'disinfecting' the affected area might not be one which has your own best interests at heart. They used a nuke on the infected town at the end of *Return of the Living Dead*. I'm just saying...

5. Location, location, location: Where you hole yourself up will have a major bearing on whether you survive for a few minutes or a few days. TV studios, I would have thought, are not the most auspicious or secure environments when

you're trying to stave off a veritable tidal wave of worm-infested crazies. A shopping mall, as is well known, is ideal; the queues at Starbucks can be expected to be substantially shorter and you can have your pick of the Blu-Ray discs out of HMV. But there won't be any power to operate your HD TV. D'oh!

However, if you and your friends are fortunate enough to find a fully-stocked and easily-secured shopping mall, try to make sure you're in America; you won't find any gun stores at Silverburn or Bluewater. Secondly, be choosy about who you allow into your little community: loud-mouthed misogynists with violent or psychopathic tendencies and the words 'Author's message: who are the real monsters?' tattooed across their foreheads should be asked to apply in writing, with a 28-day cooling-off period recommended before acceptance.

6. Is the zombie plague confined to Blighty (*28 Days Later*), or is it international (all the others). If the latter, then I'm afraid you're screwed. Make the most of the few days of life you have left before you're either eaten alive or shot by that bloke with the tattoo on his forehead – you know, that tattoo you never got round to reading? If the former, you may be saved, eventually, by Johnny Foreigner or, more likely, Billy Yank who has, after all, more experience in this sort of thing.

An important general point to bear in mind is that the dearly departed-and-returned are still, to all intents and purposes, dead. Okay, they're running/walking about attacking the living and groaning and being a post-modern metaphor and stuff, but they are nevertheless dead. That means time is on your side. Two words: flesh rots. Especially the eyes. So a few days into the ZomFest you'll find it much easier to negotiate your way past the buggers, although you'll still have to outrun them, at least until their ligaments decompose properly. They'll just start to run into things after a while, providing much-needed slapstick in the midst of a generally humourless situation. And not being willing to attend their regular six-monthly dental check-ups, their teeth will also not last long.

That's about all the advice I can offer, I'm afraid. It's all pretty depressing, but on the plus side, you won't have to go into work again or sit through *Heartbeat* on a Sunday evening.

And whenever the tell-tale signs that signal the onset of the ZomFest – oddly vague reports on the BBC News channel about 'serious incidents throughout the country' accompanied by shots of fires filmed from the air – start to occur, take solace in the fact that the end will come bewilderingly quickly: somewhere between 90 and 120 minutes, in my experience.

Okay, I'm off to lie down in a dark room now...

The End of Time, part 2
Published: January 3, 2010

David Tennant had just made his final appearance as the Doctor in a special two-part Christmas episode of Doctor Who. *As if Christmas isn't already an emotional time for me*

Forty years.

Forty years ago to this very day, my five-year-old self sat in our living room in Beith and watched my very first full episode of *Doctor Who*.

And yes, it was scary! No hiding behind the sofa for me, oh no, no, no. As a featureless, silent dummy with a gun hidden in its plastic wrist pursued its victim through the woods, I exited the living room altogether, using the presence of a box of Gypsy Creams as an excuse to venture into the kitchen, re-emerging only after the action on screen had reverted to a less nightmare-inducing scene.

Not only was this the very first *Doctor Who* adventure broadcast in colour, it was also the first starring Jon Pertwee. And he was *my* Doctor. Always has been, always will be.

That's not to say that I have no affection or admiration for other actors who have taken up the part; Tom Baker was probably the best Doctor ever. It's just that he came along when I was too old to be scared by the programme. And I loved to be scared. Still do.

Which brings me to the departure two days ago of David Tennant's tenth Doctor. He was an inspired choice to play the part, wasn't he? I vividly recall hearing the news, after just one episode of the rebooted *Who* had been broadcast in 2005, that Christopher Eccleston was packing it in at the end of the season. The news provoked hysterical sobbing in middle-aged men throughout the length and breadth of my house, and a consequent sneering contempt for them displayed by their wives. Or wife...

Anyhoo, the same news bulletin held out a grain of hope that the future was not as grim as first feared: speculation was rife that the star of Russell T. Davies's previous BBC drama, *Casanova*, would take over from Eccleston. This was confirmed a few short weeks later and, on 18 June 2005, the ninth Doctor 'died', to be replaced by the gurning countenance of the young Scottish actor.

For four years he's played the part – longer than the average tenure of other actors playing the role. Only Tom Baker and Pertwee lasted longer (if we don't count Sylvester McCoy's disastrous reign as lasting from 1987, when he took over, right up until Paul McGann's appearance in the 1996 TV movie; the series was cancelled in 1989).

So before I offer some critical remarks about part 2 of 'The End of Time', let me offer a balance to some of the criticism that Davies has endured during his time as *DW*'s showrunner. Yes, his writing wasn't always consistent. He too often relied on incomprehensible McGuffins to get the Doctor out of situations he himself had created. He wrote some real stinkers: 'Fear Her' in season two springs readily to mind, as does the finale of season three, when the Master is defeated in an entirely unsatisfactory way.

Yet one of the reasons for the criticisms was that he himself raised the bar so high when the series was relaunched in 2005. RTD is a fan, and he understands what made *DW* such a success in the first place. More to the point, he understood why it was eventually cancelled. The ridiculous scripts, lamentable acting, and plots that tried to be more clever than scary and ended up as neither. The producer who presided over the death of the 'classic' *Doctor Who* was Jon Nathan-Turner, a man who simply didn't understand what the show was supposed to be. When it was cancelled it deserved to be; it deserved to be put out of its misery.

RTD was the anti-Nathan-Turner, reversing the damage done by his predecessor and breathing new life into a beloved show. Sometimes the critics overlooked how successful he was. How quickly we forget how grateful we were that he was appointed to resurrect the show in the first place. Because he is one of the best TV writers in the country and he produced, even at its weakest points, something that was high quality and wonderfully entertaining.

But let's talk about Friday's episode which saw the introduction, in its last few seconds of Matt Smith's Doctor.

It had all the hallmarks of a typical RTD story: an epic notion (the return, not just of the Time Lords, but the planet Gallifrey itself in Earth's orbit), improbable solutions and more mysticism and prophecies than you can shake a sonic screwdriver at.

How could a single bullet fired into a computer panel foil the Time Lords' plans to take over Earth? How could a diamond thrown by Rassilon (for it was he) at a hologram of Earth actually find its way into the Master's back yard? How could the isolation chamber in the mansion be made of Vinvocci unbreakable glass? Why had Donna's mother and fiancé, having turned into the Master the day before, not moved from the kitchen by the time the process was reversed by the Time Lords? What was the 'defence mechanism' used by Donna to escape the pack of ravenous Masters in the alleyway?

Nevertheless, it was wonderful to watch, and it had some golden moments: the realisation that the Master's own warped personality was a deliberate construct of the Time Lords themselves, the Doctor and the Master each choosing to fight the Time Lords rather than each other; Wilf doing a *Millennium Falcon* on the pursuing missiles.

And of course, there was David Tennant, whose performance was breathtaking. His angry bitterness at Wilf for getting himself trapped in the isolation chamber was just amazing. His plaintive cry of 'I don't want to go!' as his regeneration drew near was positively heartbreaking.

So, on the whole, a brilliant but deeply flawed episode, and one well worth watching again.

Davies and Tennant will be deeply missed and they have both contributed massively to the success of the popular myth that is *Doctor Who*. I'm prepared to be proved wrong, but I expect that Steven Moffat and Matt Smith will pick up the baton and take the series to new heights.

Chasing the Doctor

Published: February 1, 2010

This next post contains the picture caption of which I am most proud.

When you're a football fan, nobody thinks it's at all immature or weird to want to meet one of your footballing heroes. I mean, you should have seen the number of grown men queuing up to have their photos taken with Kenny Dalglish a few weeks ago in the Sports and Social.

But if kickerball isn't your bag, if your cultural and recreational tastes lie in an altogether different direction – say, *Doctor Who*, for example – then you're just a geek, aren't you?

Well, I'm a geek.

The whole of my life I've been a *Who* fan (or 'Whovian' for those of the anorak-appreciating tribe). And for much of that time, I've been keen to meet an actor who has played the lead role of everyone's favourite Time Lord. The first chance I got was in 1979, when Tom Baker was scheduled to appear in John Menzies in Buchanan Street, Glasgow, to sign copies of the new *Doctor Who* paperback, *The Horror of Fang Rock*. And I was *so* desperate to go. Only problem was, I had made one of my rare trips to Glasgow just a week earlier and spent all my spare cash on *Trigan Empire* books and what-have-you. My mum point blank refused to bail me out and I could tell that no tantrum, however impressive, was going to change her mind (interesting point: in his *Desert Island Discs* appearance over Christmas, David Tennant revealed that he had, in fact attended that very signing).

The next opportunity to meet a Doctor didn't arise until many, many years later – 2007, in fact, when I attended the press preview of the Christmas special, *Voyage of the Damned*, at the London Science Museum. I met many other *Who* actors – John Sim, Elisabeth Sladen, Tony Head, Russell Tovey and Russell 'the T' Davies himself – but despite having been tipped off by Steven Moffat that Peter Davison was due to make an appearance, he didn't show. And David Tennant left pretty shortly after the Q&A which followed the screening, so two of them escaped in the same evening.

A few short months later, I was hosting a table at a Labour Party gala fundraiser dinner, when who should appear on stage to introduce the Prime Minister but the tenth Doctor himself, another son of the manse. After his speech, I decided I would wait until the unseemly gaggle of women fans (honestly! Have they no pride?) around his table dispersed before casually sauntering over and introducing myself. And then, just as I was about to make my move, he was led from the room and disappeared into his waiting car. Damn. It.

The next near miss was the very worst, most galling of all. In April or May 2008 I was texted by Steven Moffat, who had just been announced as Russell T. Davies's replacement as showrunner of *Doctor Who*. Would Carolyn and I like to join him and his friends at his house to watch the broadcast of *Silence in the Library*, his latest writing contribution to the series? Well, of course we would! Unfortunately, Carolyn and I were in Glasgow and not, as Steven had assumed, in London, so we had to turn down the invitation. A few weeks later Steven told me it was a pity we couldn't make it because 'you would have enjoyed meeting David and Georgia'. That would be David Tennant and Georgia Moffatt, who played the eponymous role in the season four episode, *The Doctor's Daughter,* and also happens to be Peter Davison's real-life daughter. I could have barfed!

And then, last autumn, Steven and his wife, Sue, came for dinner at the Commons. 'We've just left Matt,' said Steven in passing, 'Matt' being Matt Smith, who will play the eleventh Doctor. 'Would he want to join us for dinner, do you think?' I asked as nonchalantly as I could manage. 'I'll ask him,' said Steven, and I did not object to his using his mobile phone in the Strangers' restaurant, even though it's strictly against the rules. 'He would have liked to but he's on his way home now,' said Steven with a shrug. Hmm.

And then last week, finally, at long bloody last, this happened:

He was part of a lobby of Parliament by members of the Performers' Alliance, and of course I took my chance.

Inevitably, he was lovely – very approachable and patient, though I'm sure slightly baffled that so many MPs (note: not just me!) were behaving like fanboys.

It's taken more than thirty years, but at least that's another thing crossed off of my 'bucket list'.

'And that's one I took of you emptying your bins outside your house...'

Pictures by Kerry McCarthy MP

Labour: new and other

Thoughts on opposition: it's rubbish

Published: May 24, 2008

Some Labour-supporting blogs are advising a decisive shift to the left in order to shore up our core support. This would be electoral suicide. To pursue this path would be to admit that Labour's natural place is in opposition.

Here's my philosophy on opposition: it's rubbish. New Labour is not a PR strategy, it's a political philosophy, one that has delivered more success – in delivery and in electoral success – than at any other point in Labour's history. It's based on the premise that governments should, in fact, govern for the whole nation, and not just those who voted for them, and far less just their core electors.

Most of those calling for a left-wing realignment are the same people who have always been calling for a left-wing realignment. Our response to them should be the same as it has always been: we will not abandon the coalition that brought us to power in 1997, even if, for the time being, much of that coalition has abandoned us.

Lurch to the left? Gosh, that's original!

Published: June 2, 2008

That Lib Dem-supporting columnist John Harris (no relation) is today calling for a lurch to the left to meet the challenge of Cameron's new Conservatives. He attacks John Hutton for his 'fierce hostility to any calls for new employment regulation' and then states: 'Given that Harriet Harman won last year's deputy leadership election by affecting a tack leftwards, and 92 per cent of Labour donations are now coming from the unions, this kind of heresy will no longer fly.'

Harris adds: 'What might have seemed the right Labour path for the 1990s is increasingly looking like the wrong course for the early twenty-first century. In the wake of the credit crunch, New Labour's obeisance to the free market is looking very rusty indeed.'

Well, two obvious questions first: hasn't Harris been a constant critic of New Labour under Blair? So there's nothing new here; he would have said exactly the same thing three years ago in the wake of the third general election victory that Blair and New Labour delivered.

Second, is he saying that Cameron is currently popular because he's so different from Blair and New Labour, or because he's perceived as the same? Is Labour losing support to the Tories because we're not left wing enough? (Okay, that's three questions, I know.)

I don't suggest that there shouldn't be a debate within government and the party about how we reconnect with the electorate – the whole electorate and not just Labour's so-called 'core vote'. But when people are clearly feeling the strain of rising prices, now is not the time to be quite so dismissive, as Harris is, of 'the liberal tradition for 'instinctively disliking income tax'. The electorate – all parts of it – dislike income tax. If we're to re-engage voters, we could get off to a worse start than by accepting that we share that particular opinion.

In praise of McDonald's

Published: July 13, 2008

I was particularly proud of the 'Octopussy' line in this, but no one noticed it.

This is one of the first pieces I wrote that was consciously opposed to what most people would expect a Labour MP to believe. I never once wrote anything on the blog that wasn't what I genuinely believed. And I was right. Obviously.

Just finished a Big Mac meal (and yes, I did go large). Ronnie and Reggie had their traditional Happy Meals with chicken nuggets and strawberry shakes while Carolyn had some or other vegetarian thing.

Don't get me wrong – this is not a daily, or even weekly occurrence. Everything in moderation, and all that. But the boys do love their 'happy food' as they call it. And so do I.

So why do so many people hate McDonald's? As far as I can see, they sell extremely tasty food at reasonable prices, they provide an activity and a venue that is decidedly family-friendly. More importantly, they provide employment for many people, particularly the young. And if you can get past the 'McJob' snobbery that's prevalent today, it might be recognised that McDonald's, in many communities, are an important employer. More to the point, if McDonald's were not there, those communities would be worse off.

The same is, of course, true for many fast food outlets that provide vital jobs particularly for young people, whether long or short term, and provide a popular service at the same time. The more people who can gain an understanding that 'service sector' need not necessarily mean 'second best', the better.

My only complaint is that here in Britain, the definition of 'fast', as in 'fast food', can too often be used with scant regard to the strict dictionary definition. And it can be a tad frustrating when the person serving you responds to your request for anything vegetarian with a look of utter bewilderment.

A ned's a ned, for a' that
Published: July 16, 2008

The Fabians aren't actually calling for the term 'chav' to be banned, but Iain Dale is incensed at the suggestion that we should 'tut' at those who use it.

At the risk of needlessly winding anyone up (as if!), I have some sympathy with him. For years there's been some debate in Scotland about the use of our equivalent term, 'ned', which is seen by some as offensive. Yet when you use 'ned' to describe certain individuals, it's immediately clear to whom you're referring.

The Judean People's Front, aka the Scottish Socialist Party, used to effect righteous indignation at the use by Labour of the term to describe the small minority of young people who could be described as anti-social. But no one paid much attention to the SSP, including the neds.

On a more serious note, it's surely useful to use an unflattering term to describe those whose behaviour is anti-social or destructive to their communities. And if they find it offensive, well maybe they should stop behaving like neds.

So absurd it can't be true. Can it?

Published: July 18, 2008

I am informed that Scotland no longer has Neets. No, not head lice – NEETS, young people who are Not in Education, Employment or Training. Not that the SNP 'government' has succeeded in getting them all into work or training, they've simply changed their name (allegedly).

Instead of Neets, they're now called Young Persons Requiring Holistic Empowerment Within A Safe and Nurturing Environment. Or something.

South of Carlisle, we still have Neets, but apparently the PC police took advantage of the change in administration at Holyrood last year to pounce on inexperienced new ministers and persuade them of the case that the term Neets was somehow offensive (of course).

Altogether now: 'It's political correctness gone…'

Unworthy descendants

Published: October 14, 2008

I'm not a fan of 'direct action'.

Protesters attempted to storm the Houses of Parliament last night, and a compliant media duly provided the coverage that such a cunning stunt was intended to achieve for the organisers.

Some of them, apparently, were dressed as suffragettes (the protesters, not the media, though who knows these days?). But why? Undoubtedly these women (and they were all women) believe their cause – opposition to airport expansion – is justification enough for civil disobedience, in the same way their forebears had a moral authority by virtue of their cause.

And yet...

The suffragettes took direct action because they had few alternatives: they could hardly register their unhappiness at the ballot box, could they? They fought for the right for every adult, on an equal basis, to have the same say in how the country is run. They weren't fighting for special or privileged treatment; they didn't want more of a say than anyone else – they simply wanted to move from 'one man, one vote' to 'one person, one vote'.

I doubt if those brave, self-sacrificing pioneers of democracy would be very impressed with what we saw yesterday. The attempt to break the law was self-indulgent and it was elitist – the very antithesis of what the suffragettes were hoping to achieve. Believing that your own cause is so much more important than anyone else's doesn't give you the right to try to subvert the law – a law constructed by a government elected through universal suffrage and accountable to the whole electorate, not simply to those privileged to have enough time on their hands to spend the whole of Monday in Parliament Square.

By all means protest. But don't try to convince yourself that your cause is so great that it uniquely justifies breaking the law. Because somewhere there's a fascist with a grudge who may well choose to follow your example.

The ultimate insult

Published: October 25, 2008

Apparently some protesters ('You name it, we'll protest against it!') have taken time out of their busy schedules* just long enough to assault immigration minister Phil Woolas using a cream pie as an offensive weapon.

Obviously, as with all similar protests, this will now result in a change of government policy. I'm sure that afterwards, Phil must have thought: 'Well, that's really made me rethink my views – everything is so clear to me now…'

But the biggest insult is that they used vegan cream to make it. VEGAN cream! Not even some decent double or clotted! Even that horrible synthetic stuff in a can (known in Scotland as 'skooshy cream') would have been an improvement. What next? Gluing themselves to government buildings using bio-degradable super-glue? Tying themselves to earth-moving equipment using locally-resourced, organically-grown, hand-weaved reeds, perhaps?

Honestly, standards these days…

* *(cough, cough)*

The 'hey everybody, look at me!' school of protest
Published: December 8, 2008

I'm rather losing patience with the self-righteous, self-appointed guardians of our planet who, this morning, caused a number of cancellations at Stansted Airport by illegally entering a restricted area.

'But climate change is more important than obeying laws,' they will no doubt bleat when they appear in some magistrate's court somewhere in the near future. And on recent evidence, they'll have a better-than-50 per cent chance of getting off with it.

When did the rules change? When did we decide that vandals breaking into nuclear subs and occupying runways, causing havoc to thousands of ordinary people trying to go about their daily lives, who have no respect for the democratic processes of our country, are suddenly heroes?

As a minister at the Department for Transport I received word one day that I should avoid the main entrance when I returned to the office because some anti-Heathrow protesters had super-glued themselves to the glass doors. Staff and police were busy using various solvents to release them, I was informed.

'Why?' I asked. After all, there was more than one entrance to the building and if they chose to spend the weekend stuck to a glass door with no food or access to the toilet, shouldn't we respect their right to demonstrate?

Alas, my view did not prevail.

That Cameron action plan in full...
Published: January 11, 2009

According to this morning's interview with Andrew Marr, Do-Nothing's new government will make everything okay simply by virtue of being a new government.

So, to summarise, Dave will rescue the economy, repair 'Broken Britain' and reverse global warming through the implementation of the following steps:

1. Form a new government.
2. Er...
3. That's it with regard to this one.

So let's hear no more of this accusation that the Tories are the 'do nothing party', you hear me?

The Labour disease
Published: February 21, 2009

According to Guido, Douglas Alexander has followed Hazel Blears in delivering a 'rebuke' to those positioning themselves for a post-election defeat leadership contest:

> The many party staff I have met this week who, with our members, will be on the front line of that campaign, want the direction and focus of the Cabinet's efforts to

be getting Britain through the downturn and working together to secure a Labour victory. All of us should remember the words from our party's constitution, on the back of our membership card: 'By the strength of our common endeavour we achieve more than we achieve alone.' When the general election comes, securing a fourth term will be difficult but do-able. The task of securing that fourth term will require unity, effort and innovation.

Well, they'll be quaking in their boots after that tirade, eh?

It seems that my definition of 'rebuke' is different from Douglas's. But then, that's probably one of the many reasons why he's a Cabinet minister and I'm ... well, not so much.

So with that preamble, here's my own contribution to Labour's ferrets/sack interface scenario, drafted last night, before Douglas's excoriating contribution:

A friend and party colleague living in London emailed me yesterday to let me know he has resigned from the party. I won't go in to too many details, but he said that the recent briefing against Harriet Harman was, for him, the last straw.

Also yesterday we had the wonderful Hazel Blears telling the Cabinet to 'get a grip' and warning colleagues to stop positioning themselves for a post-election leadership contest.

To serve as a minister at any level of government is an incredible privilege and it is – or should be – a humbling experience. To serve as a Cabinet minister is a rare and magnificent opportunity, one that should be used to do good, and nothing else. It should not be used to brief against any other member of the Cabinet or, indeed, any other member of the government. When the media report that this government is defeatist, we should point the finger of blame at those 'comrades' who would rather tear colleagues down in off-the-record briefings to journalists than make sure their departments deliver for the people they represent.

I count as friends many journalists, some of whom have told me – privately, of course – the names of those 'Labour Party sources' who have briefed against ministers. One reporter even offered to show me the shorthand notes he had taken down during one such conversation.

Now, apparently, we have Cabinet ministers doing the same. Pathetic.

But there is a very real danger in this for all of the current Cabinet. I've no idea if reports about Harriet 'positioning herself' are accurate; I do happen to know who has been briefing against Harriet and other ministers. Not every MP has this information, so they will make a guess. They may get it wrong. The wrong ministers might be identified as culpable and will pay the price in terms of backbench support.

I genuinely believe that Labour is still in the game as far as the next election is concerned. But that is *despite* the activities of these colleagues, certainly not because of them.

To those who imagine that their personal ambitions actually matter to anyone other than themselves, who put their own success above the success of this government, I have this advice: sod off out of my party.

In a piece of wisdom that should be framed and hung in the office of every government minister, Hazel Blears said:

> Our first loyalty is to the British people. If they think we are more interested in our own jobs than theirs, they will not forgive us.

Nor should they.

Capping private wealth would be an admission of defeat

Published: August 18, 2009

There's a terrific scene in the TV adaptation of Chris Mullin's *A Very British Coup* in which the newly-elected, left-wing Prime

Minister, Harry Perkins, is catching the train to London and is asked by a journalist: 'Do you intend to abolish first class, Mr Perkins?' To which Perkins replies: 'No, I intend to abolish second class. I think everybody's first class, don't you?'

And there we have it: a template for New Labour half a dozen years before Tony Blair became leader of the Labour Party. New Labour's appeal was based on an explicit acknowledgement that success, ambition and the pursuit of wealth are all Good Things. Suddenly the taxation of the wealthier was not an end in itself but simply a necessary evil. And it was okay to want a better job, a higher income, nicer holidays, a bigger house. Voting Labour became something you did for yourself as well as for the greater good.

That's why we won.

Yesterday Compass launched a campaign for a High Pay Commission. Its inaugural statement reads:

> The crisis we find ourselves in is one significantly caused by greed. The salaries of those at the top raced away while the median wage stagnated. Inequality grew and an economic crisis ensued. The unjust rewards of a few hundred 'masters of the universe' exacerbated the risks we were all exposed to many times over. Banking and executive remuneration packages have reached excessive levels. We believe now is the time for government to take decisive action.

Fortunately, the Chancellor has already dismissed the idea. But as dog whistle politics go, it's pretty effective. After all, so many have suffered as a result of the banking crisis and no one ever lost votes by having a go at those we perceive as spoiled and arrogant rich kids. But I can't help thinking that the authors of that statement are the kind of people who might approve of attacking a Tory by-election candidate as a 'Toff' and using top hats as photo props.

When the national minimum wage (NMW) is discussed, it's often described as a concession by Tony Blair, as if it were something he had to tolerate in return for more 'New Labour' measures such as public service reform. Wrong. The NMW was as much a New Labour as an Old Labour achievement because it levelled people up. It was exactly the opposite of class warfare, which is why there is now a consensus between the two parties that it should remain regardless of who forms the next government.

I imagine the so-called High Pay Commission (I wonder how much the chairman would be paid?) would have the aim of setting a national maximum wage. I doubt if a clearer example of the politics of envy has been aired at any time in the last twelve years.

This proposal has 'securing our core vote' written all over it. Except it wouldn't, because once you've addressed the understandable anger at certain individuals' exorbitant salaries, pensions and bonuses, you're left with the principle that a Labour government is setting a ceiling on individuals' wealth. And that's not what governments should be doing, because once you've established that principle, once you've raised a few cheers by ostentatiously depriving some bankers of their bonuses, where do you go next? What do you do when the media get round to identifying the next figures of public hatred? Target them too? How far down the scale do you go? After all, multi-millionaires may not be able to justify their bonuses to the general public, but neither can civil servants earning six figures or MPs earning five justify their incomes to some of those living off benefits.

Undoubtedly, there are already those typing in the comments box to the effect that, since the government already own the banks, it has the right to intervene to limit financial rewards of those still running them. As indeed it does. But most of the banks and financial institutions aren't in the public sector. The principle that high bonuses are A Bad Thing is surely applicable across the board, whether a company is publicly or privately owned.

If government decides it can intervene in the market to dictate wages, why shouldn't it have a role in deciding other areas of corporate policy? And if it starts doing that, it might as well nationalise the… Oh. Okay, I get it now…

As disgraceful and unjustifiable as these bonuses were/are, they did not lead directly to the banks' bankruptcy. Poor lending and investment decisions and reckless risk-taking did. So although we might feel better confiscating money from rich people, the actual effect on our economy would be negligible. And making yourself feel better is a very poor motivation for policy, whatever 'the court of public opinion' might say on the matter.

And when any party starts producing policy 'to secure the core vote', it might as well write off the next election, go quietly into opposition right now and start thinking about the election after next.

Eton trifles

Published: October 3, 2009

I've tried, believe me, I've tried. But however much effort I commit, I just cannot bring myself to give a stuff about whether David Cameron was a member of the Bullingdon Club or a direct descendent of William IV or whatever.

I don't care if he has a trust fund worth millions or a cut glass accent that makes him sound like a member of central casting on a Jane Austen period drama. His class and background, the school or university he went to, who his family are connected to ... nope – zero amount of interest here. Bo-ring.

What I care about is the kind of person he is. I would have no hesitation in supporting a Labour Party leader with the same background as Cameron's, provided he had the ability to lead and the character to inspire. Similarly, I would oppose the Tory Party even if it were led by someone of a more modest background.

I don't want Cameron to become Prime Minister – not because he's posh, but because (a) he's a Tory and (b) I don't believe he is politically sincere. I think his reinvention of the Tory Party has been all about image and message and not at all about substance.

Anyway, that brings me to *When Boris Met Dave*, to be broadcast on Channel 4 next Wednesday at 9.00pm. Great controversy is expected to ensue, since this docu-drama portrays a young Cameron and Johnson at Eton and as members of the infamous 150-year-old club.

Yawn.

Surely the most important revelation that will emerge from this programme is that as a teenager, Cameron was a fan of Genesis and Phil Collins! On that fact alone, I am prepared to review my previous negative view of him. I mean, come on! No one who likes Genesis can be all bad...

How I invented New Labour
Published: November 11, 2009

Okay, I should acknowledge that T. Blair, G. Brown and P. Mandelson also helped...

But trawling through *The Herald*'s excellent online archive, I came across a piece I wrote in August 1993 – a year before Tony Blair became leader – entitled 'Labour activists and Jo Public' in which I wrote:

> While Labour continues to be seen by the electorate exclusively as a party of the poor, the weak, and the dispossessed, much of its membership is unable – or unwilling – to accept that it must be able to relate and appeal to the haves and not just the have-nots if electoral victory is to become a reality.

It was written less than a year after I left the employ of the Labour Party in Scotland (as it was known then). Apart from the surprisingly negative view I had of some of my fellow activists at the time (I was going through a bad patch, politically and personally, I seem to recall) I think my analysis has held up pretty well in the intervening sixteen years.

I come to bury the Tory Party, not praise it

Published: November 29, 2009

One of many posts in which I have to explain that I don't want to be a member of the Tory Party.

It's always nice to receive compliments for my blogging. The only problem is that I generally receive them from Tories, rather than from fellow party members.

The latest case in point is the recently-founded Tory Tavern blog, which writes:

> So, a fantastic few days blogging from Mr Harris. The landlord has one remaining nagging thought, though. With his common-sense, honest and open approach to politics, his rejection of electoral reform, his commitment to unionism, his criticism of Labour plans to raise taxes on the rich, his dislike of political correctness and his view that Gordon Brown should resign … is he sure he's in the right party?

So let's tackle those points head-on.

First off, I don't think that having a 'common-sense, honest and open approach' to politics is or should be the preserve of any one party; there are bloggers from all the main parties who subscribe to those values – and plenty who don't.

Support for the first-past-the-post electoral system is still the mainstream view among MPs and activists in the Labour Party, so supporting it publicly is hardly taking a 'maverick' stance.

As far as unionism is concerned, the Labour Party is far more committed to the Union than the modern Conservative Party is. A Tory party committed to making Scottish, Welsh and Northern Irish MPs second-class members of the Commons would be a greater threat to the United Kingdom than the SNP could ever be.

On taxes, Tony Blair and New Labour won the confidence of the electorate by persuading the country that Labour no longer believed in taxing for its own sake, that if they have to be raised at all, it should be done reluctantly, as a last resort, and to fund a specific spending commitment. That's what I – and the vast majority of Labour MPs – still believe.

My frustration with political correctness is actually illustrated by Tory Tavern's citing of it as evidence that I'm in the wrong party: why on earth must the Labour Party allow itself to fall into the trap of defending it? I haven't met a single person – of any party or none – who can defend the more witless examples of political correctness. The young boy sent home with a note to his parents revealing that he had uttered anti-German sentiments while his class was being taught about the Second World War? The student who was arrested and forced to spend the night in the cells for calling a police horse gay? And don't even start me on 'Winterfest' or 'NeutralFest' or 'Let'sMakeSureNo oneCanPossiblyBeOffendedByReferencesToChristianityFest' or whatever. No one defends that kind of nonsense, and if Labour Party members do, I've never met them.

To the above list of indictments, I should ask for my views on benefit dependency and single parents and my robust approach to asylum to be considered as more 'offences' to be taken into account. These have been portrayed by the media as being 'anti-Labour' or at least 'anti-left wing'. In fact, on the single parents issue, while I did receive some messages of support from Conservative colleagues in the Commons, I was overwhelmed by the support I received from Labour colleagues who told me it was 'about time' someone said what I said.

I don't specifically adopt these views in order to drive up traffic on this blog or to earn praise from right wingers. I believe that the views I hold are shared not only by the vast majority of what most people understand to be Labour's 'core vote', but by the vast majority of the wider electorate. And I espouse those views because (a) I believe they are right, and (b) I believe Labour would be more popular if more of its representatives at every level were to voice them.

And that's the whole point: I want Labour to win the general election and to stay in government, because that, in my opinion, would be in the best interests of my country and my constituents.

So, yes, Tory Tavern, I *am* in the right party. And if I had my way, your party would have a longer term in opposition ahead of you than behind you.

A word from our sponsors
Published: January 28, 2010

Finding myself, once again, at odds with the rank and file – and even with some of the leadership – of my party.

Oh. What a surprise – I'm in disagreement with Compass. Again.

This time, I'm stepping up to defend the principle of product placement in TV drama. Compass are upset because it's all about the kids, see? Apparently the ban on product placement during children's programmes is all very well, but most children's daily diet of TV is gleaned from non-specific children's programming. So if, as expected, the Department of Culture, Media and Sport's recent consultation leads to a policy decision to allow TV companies to sell screen time to well-known brands, then parents will be forced to feed junk food and alcohol to their under-fives. Or something.

(Sorry, I just took a break from my keyboard to pour myself a refreshing glass of Diet Coke©; it really is the Real Thing© – and delicious too... Anyway, where was I? Ah, yes...)

So, if Compass have their way, production companies would have a major source of income denied to them, forcing them to rely ever more heavily on the TV licence payers. Domestically-produced TV drama would become as rare as a Scottish Tory and we would have thousands of redundancies in the industry. And for what? Some disputed research in twenty years' time that may or may not tell us that children's health has improved and that the banning of product placement on non-children's television may well have played a part, even though no one can say exactly how much of a part or confirm definitively whether it had any affect at all.

Result!

(Excuse me a second: I have to vacuum the living room before Carolyn gets back. Fortunately, I have a Dyson© DC25 whose revolutionary bag-less design makes all those household chores a breeze…)

Would it be so hard for our 'think tanks' on the left to come up with policy ideas that stopped banning stuff? Why are they so keen to feed the (entirely justified) accusation from the right that too many on the left want to restrict individual choice, and don't trust adults to make their own choices? Don't they realise that if all these ideas were actually adopted by a Labour government or became part of a Labour manifesto, you'd hear the likes of Tim Montgomerie and Iain Dale high-fiving from miles away?

I reject absolutely the notion that there is anything remotely right wing about wanting to leave lifestyle decisions to grown-ups. To claim that a desire to respect individual choice is incompatible with being left wing is… well, bloody stupid, actually. And those of us on the left who still have the sense to speak out about such nonsense do so not because we seek the approval of Tory commenters, but because we want Labour to be successful as a political party and as a government.

Now, I'm going to relax for the rest of the evening, and I'll start with the delicious aroma of Tassimo© coffee – real coffee, but instant – and perhaps a little bit of that sweet … oh, what's it called? Can't remember, but I know for a fact that one a day helps you work, rest *and* play. So it can't be bad.

A racist writes

Published: September 4, 2010

I am a racist.

I had no idea up until this morning, when I was informed that my racism has manifested itself in a particularly ugly act of race-oriented bigotry and vindictiveness: I have not made a financial contribution to Diane Abbott's leadership campaign.

I know! I can barely write about it, I am so ashamed.

It gets worse: I actually couldn't care less that Diane's campaign is funds-starved. I really couldn't. It just doesn't take up much thinking time.

And even worse – and I might as well sign up to the BNP right now – even though I have already stated that I wouldn't bother using my second, third or subsequent preference votes in the leadership election, if I had chosen to use them all ... (*deep breaths*) ... *I would have given Diane my fifth preference vote*. Because any of the other candidates would make a preferable leader to her. There – I've said it.

Now, in my defence, that is a position based exclusively on political considerations. It's a conclusion that many, many members of the Labour Party – both rank and file as well as MPs – will have come to by now.

And we're all racists. Yup. Every one of us.

You know how I know that? Because Sir Ian Blair says so. In his article for *The New Statesman*, headlined 'Racism is alive and kicking', he says:

> How, for instance, can Labour Party members not be outraged about the lack of donations to Diane Abbott's leadership campaign?

And I have to be honest: I'm not outraged at all.

So my being racist is the only sensible conclusion to reach, isn't it? Either that, or Sir Ian is talking out of his backside.

The case for the defence

Published: October 25, 2010

Although I didn't think it at the time, this post, written in frustration at the lack of support from people I knew to think exactly along the same lines as me, spelled the beginning of the end of the blog.

For many years I've enjoyed a reputation for being a 'right winger' in the Labour Party, whatever that term even means nowadays.

Some of my detractors will even go so far as suggesting I defect to the Conservative Party, so far from the Labour Party orthodoxy have I wandered. I think I'm supposed to be offended by such comments, but I'm not sure. Must check that out at some point...

So, at the risk of sounding a tad defensive on the point, let's examine the evidence for the prosecution:

1. I'm opposed to benefit dependency and think it's a bad idea for teenagers to become parents.
2. I support renewal of Trident.
3. I oppose a 'High Pay Commission'.
4. I support the removal from the UK of failed asylum seekers.
5. I supported the invasion of Iraq. And still do.
6. I supported anti-terrorism measures such as 'control orders' and 42-day detention. And still do.
7. I supported keeping the top rate of tax at 40 per cent and see higher taxes as a necessary evil, rather than as a good thing in itself.

There are other issues, undoubtedly, which opponents might wish to place a 'right-wing' label on, simply because they disagree with them and they consider themselves left wing. So, may I request that opposition to voting reform and to British membership of the euro be taken into account?

And now the defence:

1. **I'm opposed to benefit dependency and think it's a bad idea for teenagers to become parents.** Ah, well, y'see, everyone's talking about the need for Labour to make a fresh appeal to our core vote. I can offer you a cast iron guarantee that this is one issue where I'm more in touch with the core Labour vote than those who disagree with me. This is an issue that was raised on working-class doorsteps during the general election more often than immigration. Oh, and Gordon Brown agrees with me, so…

2. **I support renewal of Trident.** And so does the Labour Party, which fought the last two elections on a manifesto commitment to renew Trident.

3. **I oppose a 'High Pay Commission'.** And in government, so did the Labour Party, or at least our then (very sensible) Chancellor, Alistair Darling did. Holding an inquiry into the 'evils' of high pay sends out the message that we think wealth is A Bad Thing. Get real, comrades: high pay isn't the problem – low pay is.

4. **I support the removal from the UK of failed asylum seekers.** Labour Party/Labour government policy. I hate the expression, but this really is a 'no-brainer' (memo to self: hunt down and kill whoever invented that phrase. But only after you've checked on whether the suggestion you defect to the Tories is intended as an insult.) What's the alternative? To allow every asylum seeker to live in the UK irrespective of his/her background? That's just silly, that is.

5. **I supported the invasion of Iraq. And still do.** As did most Labour MPs, and probably a majority of party members at the time. My 'crime' appears to be that I haven't recanted. Ed and I will just have to agree to differ on that one.

6. **I supported anti-terrorism measures such as 'control orders' and 42-day detention. And still do.** When 9/11 happened, we all accepted the world had changed. Many people decided that, with the passage of time, they might have over-reacted. They didn't. There are bad people out

there who want to kill us, not because we invaded a Muslim country but because we don't share their values. They have to be stopped.

7. **I supported keeping the top rate of tax at 40 per cent and see higher taxes as a necessary evil, rather than as a good thing in itself.** Again, a manifesto commitment that may have been more tolerated than enthusiastically supported by the party. Nevertheless, a policy that we should have kept to.

Now that I've written it down, a pattern emerges: I'm considered insufferably right wing because I actually believe in what the last Labour government did. I wasn't just going along with it out of self-interest – I genuinely thought we were doing the right thing and that I should defend it.

Perhaps my mistake was that I didn't send out the correct 'signals' that, although I was voting for all this stuff, I wasn't, deep down, very happy with the 'direction' in which the government was going. Maybe, with my party back in opposition, where it has always felt most comfortable, I should pretend that I didn't actually mean to vote the way I did, that I was forced by those nasty, mean government whips to do what they told me.

Alas, 'twas not so. I'll just have to throw myself on the mercy of the court.

The end

A blessed relief

Published: November 15, 2010

Is it just me or does every blogger consider, in advance, what title he'll give to the last post he'll ever write?

I considered 'The last post' but dismissed it as too predictable. 'So long and thanks for all the comments' would have stuck with the whole *Hitchhiker's Guide to the Galaxy* shtick (*And Another Thing* being the most recent title in the 'trilogy').

Instead I've gone for the above, partly because that's how it feels, partly because it's a nod to Tony Blair's comments, on announcing that he had been persuaded to stand down as Prime Minister, that the looming Trades Union Congress would be his last. 'As much a relief for them as for me,' he added, wonderfully, reminding those of us watching how crazy we were to rid ourselves of his services.

But I digress. I love blogging because I love writing. I love politics, I love the Labour Party, I love writing about Labour Party politics.

But the blog has become a burden. It's taking up too much time (though not as much as some might think – I am a very fast writer), it's getting me into too many squabbles with people I have never met and are likely never to meet. And increasingly I've felt like I'm adopting stances simply for the sake of being confrontational and provoking a row.

Basically, the bottom line: blogging is having a negative effect on my personal, family and political life for reasons too many and complicated to recount.

I've allowed this blog to define me politically. It's done the job pretty accurately – I'm acknowledged as a dyed-in-the-wool Blairite, a point that would perhaps have been open to debate had I never taken to the web. But I've become a blogger who is also an MP rather than a politician who blogs, and that was never the aim.

I like to think I've managed to produce, over the last two and a half years, an entertaining, well-written site which has, perhaps, encouraged at least some of you to look at politicians in a new light, as people who have interests outside the narrow sphere of policy and the chamber of the House of Commons. As human. Mostly.

Thank you so much for reading and for commenting. I really do value every single person who has taken the trouble to read what I've produced. If I've managed to provoke a reaction or two along the way, great – especially if that reaction has been laughter.

But now it's time to ride off into the sunset, Macbook in my saddle, and hand over to those less jaded and less cynical.

Adios.

And another thing...

Published: November 16, 2010

I won't make a habit of writing new blog posts in order to explain why I've given up blogging, but I really feel I need to assert a few truths here.

I just did an interview for BBC World Service who, believe it or not, wanted to discuss why I'd given up. Having thought a bit more about my reasons overnight, I said something which I didn't mention in last night's post: I want to see Labour win the next election and I want to make some kind of contribution to that victory, even if that contribution is simply shutting my face. As a supporter of the policies of the last Labour government, I am out of step with Ed and some of his own views – on Iraq, taxation, electoral reform, tuition fees, to name a few. As my mum used to say (actually she didn't but she probably should have), if you can't say something nice, don't say anything at all.

This response was taken as an indication that I have been leant on by the party to stop the blogging. I don't think MPs should use words like 'bullshit' on a publicly available blog, and I've always tried to be careful not to lower the tone in such a way, so I won't say 'bullshit' now. But what a load of b******t.

But what's provoked me to make this last and final post (honest) is Mike Smithson's question – which I trust will feature in John Rentoul's ongoing and successful series of posts entitled 'Questions to which the answer is no' – 'Has Tom Harris fallen victim to Ed's new assertiveness?'

Never, at any point in the whole of my blogging career – including the period when I was a minister – has anyone in the Labour Party asked me to stop blogging. Not once. The last conversation I had with Ed M ended with him telling me: 'Keep up the blogging.'

In fact, the only thing that could have persuaded me to keep up the blogging would have been if any senior member of the party had 'instructed' me to give it up. That would have been fun.

So, no, Mike – there's no conspiracy to gag me. The Boris Johnson poster which Mike predicted might cause me trouble has done nothing of the sort; I've received only congratulations from Labour parliamentary colleagues for it and for the point I was making.

Just thought I should clarify that one.

And that really is it this time.

Epilogue

I got fed up, it's as simple as that. As I say in my brief profile over at Dale and Co., Iain Dale's new multi-contributor blogging platform, I blogged for two and a half years 'until the pressure of being entirely sensible and right all the time became too much'.

Six months after Labour's 2010 defeat seemed an appropriate time to quit. *'And Another Thing...'* belonged to a particular era, both in my life and in the life of the Labour government. By November 2010, Gordon had walked off into the sunset, my party had a new leader and we were very firmly back where Labour has always felt most comfortable: opposition.

I had one unbreakable rule while I blogged: what's said in the tearoom stays in the tearoom. The Members' Tearoom in the Commons is where all the proper politics are conducted: secrets shared, gossip digested, conspiracies hatched. Worried that colleagues would simply not wish to speak to me anymore lest their indiscretions appeared online a few minutes later, I established the Golden Rule to set their minds at ease.

But since I'm no longer a blogger, I'll share one discussion to which I was privy in spring 2011.

You generally find that MPs remain closest to colleagues who were first elected on the same day. The 2001 intake of Labour MPs considers itself a pretty gregarious bunch. And we were at first – having regular Monday evening meals together for the first couple of years after we were elected.

But that relaxed comradeship suffered a blow during the September 2006 coup when seventeen of the thirty-eight MPs who arrived in the Commons for the first time in 2001 signed that letter asking Tony to resign. Subsequently, I was often (but not always) keen to avoid awkward conversations and confrontations over that unhappy episode. I would prefer to change the subject if it looked like reminiscences about the coup might sour a previously agreeable evening.

I was with Frank Roy, the blunt-spoken Motherwell MP who kept his job as the Scottish whip throughout Gordon's premiership despite being a staunch Blairite, and Iain Wright, the Hartlepool MP who, in September 2006, didn't sign the letter but did resign as Parliamentary Private Secretary (PPS) to health minister Rosie Winterton in protest at the threat to a local hospital.

We were joined by a couple of others, Chris Bryant among them. I can't recall how the matter was raised, but suddenly Frank was making comments about the coup and Chris's role in it. They weren't particularly aggressive comments, but Frank, despite being a genuinely nice person, would probably find it difficult to avoid making expressions of love sound threatening.

It was left to me to pour oil on troubled waters. 'Oh, well, at least everything turned out fine in the end, eh?'

To which Iain Wright responded by checking his watch and pretending to get up, saying, 'Oh, look at the time – I need to get back to my ministerial off- ... Oh.'

Well, quite.

Tom Harris
July 2011